THE POCKET
OF A SEN

The Pocket Diary of a SENCO spans a typical school year and includes hopeful and often humorous diary entries that share the authentic aspirations, joys and frustrations of championing inclusion and working in the role of a SENCO.

Grounded in real-life experiences and day-to-day practice, Pippa McLean describes the experiences of a SENCO and the reality of SEND provision in school, drawing out the personal characteristics and values that schools can foster to support inclusive practice and nurture positive relationships between children, parents and colleagues. Diary extracts across the months range from 'Be ready to hit the road', 'Be gentle on yourself', to 'Be a culture builder' and 'Be an advocate'. Each entry is followed by reflective questions and space for the reader to jot down their own thoughts, as well as 'monthly musings' to support their own professional development.

Written in a truly conversational style, this essential pocket diary captures the reality of SEND provision in schools and will be relatable to many. It is valuable reading for SENCOs, teachers, support staff and trainees who wish to enrich their learning around inclusive practice and engage reflectively within their busy lives.

Pippa McLean has been a teacher and SENCO for many years, working in a number of mainstream primary schools across the South-East of England during her career. She has written regularly for publications including *nasen Connect* and has a passion for inclusion. Pippa loves investing in children and families and encouraging others to do the same, something that is seen in her commitment to school communities and other local community projects.

THE POCKET DIARY OF A SENCO

AN HONEST GUIDE TO THE ASPIRATIONS, FRUSTRATIONS AND JOYS OF CHAMPIONING INCLUSION IN SCHOOLS

Pippa McLean

Routledge
Taylor & Francis Group

LONDON AND NEW YORK

Designed cover image: © Getty Images

First published 2023
by Routledge
4 Park Square, Milton Park, Abingdon, Oxon OX14 4RN

and by Routledge
605 Third Avenue, New York, NY 10158

Routledge is an imprint of the Taylor & Francis Group, an informa business

© 2023 Pippa McLean

British Library Cataloguing-in-Publication Data
A catalogue record for this book is available from the British Library

ISBN: 978-1-032-36780-4 (hbk)
ISBN: 978-1-032-36781-1 (pbk)
ISBN: 978-1-003-33375-3 (ebk)

DOI: 10.4324/9781003333753

Typeset in Palatino and Scala Sans
by Apex CoVantage, LLC

Contents

Contents

About the author

Pippa McLean

Pippa has been a teacher and SENCO for many years. She grew up and cut her teeth in teaching in East London and has been a teacher and/or SENCO in several mainstream primary schools across the South East of England over the years. Her most recent SENCO post of nearly ten years has been in an infant and nursery school.

She has always had a passion for inclusion and knows something of the hard work, joys and frustrations along the way. She loves investing in children and families and encouraging others to do the same. Her love for people is seen in her commitment to school communities and other local community projects, and she has a heart to see people thrive.

Pippa loves a good book, a good walk and a good meal around a table with friends and family.

She and her husband have three children and are considering getting a dog.

Email: hello@pippamclean.com

Acknowledgements

There are so many people to thank . . . so many people who have invested in me over the years and have shaped me to be the person I am today. Many of you will continue to walk with me and shape me into the person I will be tomorrow and the rest of my days. The bottom line is that I love people in all their wondrous diversity, and that is something of your doing. So, thank you.

There are so many places to thank . . . places I've visited, places I've lived, and the amazing place of the London Borough of Newham where I was pretty much born and grew up. Places that have shone with the bright variety of culture as well as the nitty gritty of everyday life. They're places that from the very beginning have borne in me a passion for inclusion.

To all the children and families I've journeyed with over the years . . . thank you.
It's been a privilege to work with you and walk alongside you. In every conversation I hope I've conveyed something of my heart as well as my mind along the way . . . and in the telling of my own story, I hope I've echoed something of yours.

To all you wonderful colleagues both past and present, in a variety of different schools throughout my teaching and SENCO career . . . thank you.
Thank you for your continued hard work and commitment, and for your passion. We've learnt, laughed, and cried hard together, and I hope you've seen something of my heart.

To all my friends who encouraged me to tell this story even when I felt sure it's been told before . . . thank you.

Thank you for reading endless excerpts and urging me to keep on telling my story from the heart.

To all my family . . . thank you.
Thank you for giving me the time and space to put my heart and mind to this. Thank you for everything.

Introduction

It's all about hearts and minds. When it comes to championing inclusion you can't have one without the other. I think you can be a good SENCO (Special Educational Needs Coordinator), teacher, Learning Support Assistant or any other kind of educational practitioner if you think hard, work hard and put your mind to it. But I think you can be a *really* good one if you engage both your heart and your mind. Bringing both communicates to everyone that you're not just going through the motions or ticking boxes; that the child in your class is not just a name or a number or an element of data that needs to progress . . . that ultimately you care. If your heart's not in it there's something wrong. It just becomes functional.

The steady beating of the heart keeps everything else working, creates the rhythm for the outworking of all the other body parts, all the other functions. It's the stability, the background beat, the facilitator of oxygen to everywhere else. If our hearts stop, we're in trouble. Without the heart stuff, the mind loses focus . . . purpose . . . energy.

Some would say we should keep our hearts out of it. Keep them well out of the way, well-guarded, for the sake of self-preservation . . . that we need to do this to survive in education, to be in it for the long haul. Some would say that even allowing our hearts into the matter is somehow 'unprofessional'. I hear the warning, but I'm unsettled by it. Yes, we need to maintain boundaries around our work, because otherwise it can so easily consume us, but there's something powerful about investing our hearts into something. It communicates value to those we work with . . . children, parents, families, and colleagues alike. It communicates that we are invested in those in our care, and that they matter. . . . Children and families of children with additional and special educational needs need to know this, need to *feel* this, because all too often their experience in society is one of not mattering, not being seen, not being heard.

This is a book for SENCOs and teachers and Learning Support Assistants, office staff and site staff and anyone who works in an educational setting, because inclusion is all of our business. Inclusion is the ethos, culture and environment we create, it's the language we use, it's our heart and mind attitude, it's our hands and feet practice. If you're a SENCO looking for something to help you with provision-mapping or evaluating your whole school strategy or the impact of your interventions and their cost effectiveness, then this is not the book for you. Nor is it about many of the other things we as SENCOs oversee or coordinate. It's not so much a how-to-do book, but a how-to-be book. It's a book about who we are as practitioners, and what we bring to the role, to the team, to the families and children we work with.

As practitioners in schools, we're always reflecting on our practice, whether that be the quality of our teaching, children's progress and learning, the effectiveness of deploying and working with other adults, and outcomes for children and families. You name it, we reflect on it. But what if we also give time and space to focus our reflection on who we are and what we bring to our daily interactions with others: children, parents and colleagues? What if this has a far greater impact than we realise? Or what if we know this of course but we just lose sight of it from time to time in the frantic pace of our roles? When it comes to reflecting on our practice, what if it's actually more important to recognise who we are and the relationships we build? What if this is fundamentally more important than all our experience or subject expertise or any other valuable contribution we bring? What if, as the old adage goes, we really are the most important resource in the room?

My hope is that my experiences as a SENCO will resonate with yours, in whatever capacity you work within a school. I want you to feel like you're not alone. Because with the challenges of championing inclusion you can sometimes feel like you are even though you're working alongside and with others who are doing exactly the same thing. It's strange how you can be *with* so many people and yet sometimes feel on your own. I want you to remember that there are hundreds and thousands of people like you and me who are doing this very same thing day in day out, facing the same challenges and frustrations, as well as joys and rewards as we do this thing together. Championing . . . it brings to mind cheering each other on, like the crowd lining the streets of a marathon and waving their flags, like fellow runners sharing the road, encouraging each other to keep going when it feels like a long hard slog; celebrating together each time it feels like we've crossed a mini finishing line; fellow companions who know that feeling of being parched, desperate for the next water station, who know the relentless one foot in front of the other hitting of the roads; who know when you get your breath sucked right out of you when you hit the wall, who experience the unevenness of the tarmac, the steep incline, the sometimes gasping for air, each unknown bend of the road; fellow runners who smile and know of the joys, and what joys!!

My hope is that this little diary gives us time to reflect on the wonder and down-to-earth reality of championing inclusion. It speaks of a typical year in a mainstream school. It speaks of who we are as we go about our daily lives in schools. It champions the people we are and hope to be. It highlights characteristics and attitudes that are crucial to our roles but often go unmeasured or unacknowledged. It highlights the flexibility, resilience, compassion, creativity and countless attributes we show on any given day as we invest in the children and families in our care.

We can probably all recall teachers or support staff from our own childhood who impacted us greatly, either for the better or for worse. Memories, encounters and conversations that brought us life and stay with us to this day, or interactions that caused us to shrink a little inside and wound us even now. The person that we are, may have the greatest impact on those around us. No pressure! But the reality is we leave behind a legacy with everyone we meet and work with, children, parents and colleagues. We leave behind how people felt when we were in the room, the values that we stood for, the passion that we had, the resilience that we showed. It impacts individuals and whole school communities. It impacts the one and the many.

I know what you're thinking . . . I haven't got time to read this book! I have so many other things to do. I know. I know those feelings. I wrestle with them all the time. But you can pick this book up and read a diary entry or two in that brief moment you catch your breath at the end of a busy day, mulling over the stories and drawing parallels with your own, or you can spend more time and dig a little deeper with what you bring to the table, to the team. There are monthly musings and there's space for you to reflect and note thoughts down if you want to, so that this diary becomes something of your own too, something of an interactive space to reflect. We don't often make space for that because it feels a bit self- indulgent and we just don't have the time, or sometimes the energy, and yet as we go about the serious business of inclusion it causes us to examine our environments and practice, to examine our language and thinking deeply, and this includes examining ourselves. Our work of inclusion is totally intentional and totally all encompassing. The work is hard, the work is the best and the work is ongoing.

My hope is that this book celebrates the many, and encourages us to keep going when it's tough, to remember why we signed up in the first place and to aspire to always bring the best of ourselves. My hope is that this book acknowledges the wonder, reality and challenges that we face every day as we passionately pursue inclusive practice and celebrate the diversity of our school communities. If you're reading this as a parent, my hope is that it might help you reflect on what you want in a school, and the kind of people you want to journey with along the way, but moreover that you catch the heart of this book that simply speaks of investing in each and every child, because they're totally worth it. It's an invitation into a shared journey of hearts and minds. It's an invitation to cheer each other on.

In the process of writing of this book, I've reflected on real life experiences. Where I've used the term SENCO (Special Educational Needs Coordinator) this is sometimes referred to as SENDCO (Special Educational Needs and/or Disabilities Coordinator) in some settings. In order to protect privacy and confidentiality, children's names are entirely fictional throughout. I've written something that at times I need to read, as a reminder of bringing the best of myself, whenever I can. I've never had it all covered. I've never got it all right. But my hope is that as you read, laugh, cry, ask questions and mull things over, you'll be inspired to keep on keeping on.

HOW IT ALL STARTED

I began to write a few years ago, as a result of a really challenging time in school. We'd been working with a cohort of children with high level SEMH (Social Emotional and Mental Health) needs, and at times things felt like they and we were at crisis point. We were desperately trying to provide what the children needed, within the limited resources we had, and any attempt at seeking either short term or long-term funding seemed to be thwarted at every turn. We were trying to be creative and were seeking alternative solutions to what had begun to feel like an overwhelming situation, but decisions just didn't seem to be going our way. I needed a way to let my frustration out, to voice my exasperation with the systems and barriers that seemed to be working against us and to express my inner sense of questioning about whether we were giving these children what they really needed. So, I penned a few words . . . that's how it started.

But I guess how it really began was when I started teaching, now many years ago, as I recall the names and faces from way back then. A passion grew in me from the outset, to meet the needs of all the children in my class, each with their unique characters, strengths and needs. After lots of years in the classroom, working my hardest to help all my children to progress, I embarked on my first SENCO role. I remember a few weeks into the job, in a new school, and one of the Senior Leaders asked me what SEND qualifications I had. I had nothing 'official' . . . just lots of experience of supporting a whole host of SEND pupils in my classes over the years, and a passion for wanting the best for them. I noted her look of disapproval. It looked like I had something to prove. It's been a requirement in the UK for a while that SENCOs complete the National Award for SEN. This has helped equip SENCOs for their role. But even with this qualification, this special bit of paper, nothing really gets you ready. Nothing really prepares you for the hoops you have to jump through; the systems you have to get your head round; the mountains of paperwork to evidence everything you do; the sense of responsibility you feel for all the children. When it comes to being a SENCO, you cut your teeth in the doing of it. In the quick learning on your feet. In the feeling like you're floundering. In the balancing of the so many things to do. So, whilst the accreditation is important, what's more important is the passion. The passion to keep going when things are tough; the passion to inspire those around you; the passion to always seek the best.

Be passionate

*****

September

4th September

I loved the holidays, but last night I had that familiar 'back to school' feeling. Every year it's the same. When the alarm went off, I tried again to prepare, to get ready for my brain to go from 0–100 in a matter of seconds, but however much I try, it's always a shock to the system. Settling children in back from their break as well as those new to school is a big deal and we work hard to get it right. That means lots of preparation beforehand but also all hands-on deck in those first few weeks. After today I feel like I've already worked a full week . . . and by the weekend I know tiredness will hit me like a truck. Welcome back!

Be ready to hit the road running

*****

 REFLECT:

How ready do you feel today?

How are your resources?

If they're low, is there a small way you could top them up? What could that look like?

DOI: 10.4324/9781003333753-2

6th September

This morning, I reminded myself that I do actually really like September. It's always a shock to the system after the summer break. The keenly awaited holidays seem so long at the start, stretching out into the distance . . . so how do we always get back here so fast!? But here we are, and our bodies and minds have no time to adjust. It's a new season. A new start. A new opportunity. And we have a spring in our step!

When you're a SENCO you embark on a journey with children and parents. You know there'll be highs and lows along the way . . . that goes without saying . . . but you walk alongside, as companions on the journey, seeking to navigate the educational route together, with your teams. We're in the business of person-centred thinking and planning, with everyone working towards the best outcomes for each child and family. So, September marks another start. On your marks . . . get set . . . go! Recharged and with our feet in the starting blocks, we get ready. Ready for people.

Any good teacher or Learning Support Assistant knows that at the end of the day it's all about relationship. Yes, there's all the other stuff that goes with the job, but it's the quality of relationship that provides a secure base for learning, for trust, for belonging, for community. These are the foundations on which we build, and these are what we hope parents will glimpse from their very first interaction with our schools. From having the courtesy to return a phone call when a message has been left by an enquiring parent, the friendly greeting by office staff, an opportunity for a walkabout tour, time given to support transition planning . . . all these little things count. All these little things matter because they help to build the bigger picture. Each of our schools has a reputation in the local community; the word of mouth that goes round . . . and one of the key messages parents are asking when they're considering settings is 'Can I trust this school?' 'Can I trust these people?'

And then there's our documents. Our policies. Our websites. How do these communicate who we are? As SENCOs there's our shop window – it's our SEN Information Report on our websites. The one-stop-shop that gives parents a flavour of what our schools are like. So as well as the document stating all the legal things that it needs to, it's vital that our language also communicates something of relationship, conveying our aspirations, values and ethos. People need to know they are welcome. Both children and parents. Not a pretend welcome, with a loaded 'and have you looked at other schools in the area?', or a hesitancy and visible step backwards when a parent says their child is still in nappies. Yes, there are different provisions that may be better and best provisions for children, whether that be mainstream or specialist settings, but shamefully I have heard of some SENCOs downplaying their SEN Information Report content or style, so that they 'don't get so many'. Don't get so many what, exactly? People? We're all people. We're all unique. We all have areas of strengths and areas to develop. In our roles in schools, being person-centred is central. The clue is in the language. Not where people are off-centre, to the side or in the background . . . but central, right there in the middle. It's about relationship. And yes, there's a cost to walking alongside and journeying with people, but we have to be up for the journey.

So, September sees the start of many journeys, but for each child and family the journeys are individual. They're personal. For many the first steps are gentle, tentative, where trust needs to be built. Just like at the start of any relationship. And slowly, trust grows . . . with effort, with consistent responses and with time. Tick tock, the rhythm of the clock. Day in, day out. Week in, week out. People want to know that they're being invested in. That they matter. That their children matter. That they are not just a name on a new register, but that they are 'known', and they are valued. Yes, we'd often like trust to be fast-tracked, but that's not how it works. It comes with the daily checking-in, the step-by-step walking. It comes with the journey. So maybe a change of footwear is needed. Maybe it's less a matter of running shoes, with feet in the starting blocks, but more walking boots, ready for the terrain ahead. Ready for the change in season, ready for all kinds of weather. But let's get them on and make a start.

Be a companion

*****

9

REFLECT:

How do you feel when you look at the terrain ahead?

Who could be a companion in the journey? And how could you take a step to make that happen?

Who could you walk alongside?

7th September

There are some children that just stick in your head and your heart . . . and years down the line you find yourself thinking about them. Wondering what they're up to. Wondering how they're doing. Wondering if the things you all said and the things you all did made a difference. Today I found myself thinking about one such child. It came out of nowhere but has consumed my thinking all day. We enter the profession because we want to draw out the best in little people . . . and that caring doesn't necessarily stop on their last day with you. In schools we invest our time, effort, expertise and hearts into the children in our care. To invest in someone means there's a level of expenditure on our part. It speaks of passion, energy and devotion, to the people entrusted to us. As SENCOs we're often described as advocates . . . and rightly so. Supporting others to have a voice when all too often, systems and processes seem stacked up against them. Parents and colleagues and children want to know that we're invested in them . . . not just because it's our job and we have to . . . but because we care. It makes all the difference.

Be invested

*****

 REFLECT:

Which child sticks in your head or comes to mind now, and why?

If you feel like celebrating, sit with that feeling for a couple of minutes and enjoy it!

If you feel more difficult emotions as you think about this child, who could you share these with?

11th September

Today was one of those days where I felt completely overwhelmed for much of the day. So much to do . . . feeling like I didn't know if I was coming or going, and then right in the middle of it, a colleague came up to me and had a bit of a rant. Not *at* me, or even *about* me – but it was still a rant, and I had no real capacity to deal with it . . . and what they said stayed with me way after I got back from work. Sometimes, in the crazy busy-ness of the day, I need to remember that the people I work with are people too. Each with their own story of what they woke up to this morning, and of who they love, of what's going well and what's not. With the demands of our jobs, we can sometimes lose sight of that, until it literally seems to come up and slap you in the face. Notice the people around you. Notice what kind of days they're having, whether they're communicating it with words or not. And create a bit of time and space to ask if they're ok.

Be observant

*****

 REFLECT:

Who have you noticed today? And what did you notice?

How can you act on that noticing?

13th September

In my diary it just looked like any other termly review meeting with a parent. But it quickly became something more. I didn't do anything special . . . just created some space and asked a few questions – and then this wave of emotion poured out of this Mum. It even took her by surprise. She apologised afterwards, and I kept saying that she didn't need to – It had been an immense privilege that she'd felt safe enough to let it all out. And for a moment, time stood still, and it felt like we were on some kind of sacred ground. One entrusting another with something precious . . . and the other receiving it like a gift. And I felt proud and humbled all at the same time. Something apparently so ordinary, within moments became something so extra-ordinary. No one would be able to tell from my diary . . . but what took place was a momentous shared moment, that speaks of and builds trust all at the same time. And I knew it would stand us in good stead for the future . . . working towards the best for her daughter.

Be humbled

*****

 REFLECT:

How could you create space for a moment like this?

Who could you listen to or open up to?

19th September

Up two three four, up two three four.

His little legs were going as fast as they could carry him, but he still couldn't keep up. It was like some kind of military procession with what felt like everyone else's legs and arms marching along in unison, it's just his were out of time, and try as he might, he couldn't keep up. He couldn't get in synch.

I think that's what Archie was trying to tell me. That he just felt overwhelmed with the pace of things. That there was always a moving on to the next thing. Always a trying to keep up.

That kind of feeling when you're in it is relentless. It's exhausting.

And when children communicate it to us, we have to hear what they're saying. We have to get in step and somehow regulate the pace. We have to slow or pause or stop altogether. We have to give them time to catch their breath.

Be someone who regulates the pace

*****

REFLECT:

How does that feeling of trying to keep up when you're flailing feel for you?

Is there a child that comes to mind who might be feeling something similar right now?

How could you help to regulate the pace for them?

20th September

Today saw one of our termly SENCO Cluster meetings where SENCOs from local schools gather to discuss pressing issues or deliver training. I love them and hate them (the meetings I mean, not the SENCOs themselves!) all at the same time. We're all in the same boat I tell myself, even if our contexts look different. It's just I frequently leave these meetings with so much more to think about and do. I sometimes wonder if the title SENCO should actually stand for 'Sub-Enough, Never Completely On

15

(it)', because it's often shrouded by so many feelings of never quite doing enough, having enough, being enough, to do the job properly. And I know we're not supposed to do it all on our own. We're *coordinating* provision, within the staff team, that's where the 'co' bit of our job title comes in. Doing things *together*. It's just at times, the burden can feel heavy. The weight of responsibility, for some of the most vulnerable children in our schools; those who are Looked After or recently adopted; those at risk of exclusion; those who are very real safeguarding concerns; those with child protection orders; with mental health difficulties; young carers; those with life threatening medical conditions. I could go on . . . if you're lucky, the 'not enough' feelings just lurk in the background . . . but more often than not, they sit right there on your shoulder, or whisper in your ear, or sometimes come out of the shadows and slap you full in the face. If we're honest, lots of us feel inadequate lots of the time . . . because the job is actually just a bit too big for one. We all sometimes feel that we're not enough, and that is ok. What matters is that we press on with our best endeavours. At times they may just feel like 'endeavours' . . . like we're trying really hard. But as long as they're our best ones, that *is* enough.

Sometimes we just need to admit we're stuck. Even with years of experience doing this job, today I feel stuck. It's a 'hands up', surrender, moment. It can feel vulnerable to even say it out loud. Maybe instead it should be a 'hands up, I need help' moment, just like we encourage our children to do. So today I'm being real, honest and open. I may not feel like I'm enough, but with the help of those around me I choose to put one foot in front of the other and keep going.

Be real

*****

REFLECT:

What are your 'not enough' feelings today?
Who could you talk to about them?
Who could you go to, to ask for some encouragement?

21st September

Today I am a Super SENCO! With my flying cape and sparkly pants! Today I owned it! Everything I touched seemed to turn to gold! People were smiley and said thank you. People were appreciative of everyone's hard work. People worked as a team . . . and children were settled. Yes!!!

Be thankful for 'easier' days

*****

REFLECT:

Describe something you're thankful for today, this week

24th September

My phone just didn't seem to stop ringing today . . . can you just pop to see. . . .? . . . Please can you let me have . . .? Yes, I can, but not right now, I'm in the middle of this . . . this thing that is also important and also pressing. Sometimes I ask that my time is protected from incoming calls just so that I can get something finished, but sometimes no one else is available and the things that someone asks of you can't be done later or by anyone else. My phone rings and it's a member of staff asking for support with a child who's emotionally escalated, dysregulated . . . however you want to describe it, they're not settled and not happy. I know they won't have called if they didn't need to, but I'm in the middle of an important piece of paperwork that has a deadline and I feel like an 'interruption' is the last thing I need, and the truth is that today I feel ill-equipped for the task, but I'm the one people are asking for help. So inside, I'm saying HELP!!! . . . it's just no-one else knows.

We all want to minimise situations like these, where children are communicating a level of distress. We work hard with our planning to lessen them, but they do happen. It wouldn't be a true reflection of life in a mainstream school if we pretended them away. I sometimes wonder if when a teacher or LSA (Learning Support Assistant) calls to ask for assistance they want me to come in all guns blazing, like some Wild West cowboy figure making his entrance through a pair of saloon doors, (cue famous cowboy music); or whether I should arrive with the sound of blue sirens whirring 'nee nar nee nar' as if I'm some approaching paramedic that can heal all; or like a police officer requesting back-up over the walkie talkie. But the child is in crisis, and I've been asked to help, so on my way I'm thinking through the child's risk assessment and consistent management plan, thinking about the strategies we have in place . . . reminding myself of the consistent script or phrasing we use with this particular child on occasions like this . . . gathering information and trying to work out what has escalated this child's anxiety today, thinking what we could do differently. Sometimes just a change of personnel can help; a coming alongside can help. The situation might often still feel tricky, difficult, uncomfortable, unsettling for us all, but we work together to resolve it.

I might have a thousand and one other things to do, but for the moment, they'll have to wait.

Be interruptible

*****

REFLECT:

What is the most important thing you need to do today? Why?

Would others agree?

If it doesn't get done, would that actually be ok?

25th September

I could see the anxiety in her eyes. The not knowing. The hoping against hope that things would move quicker; that short windows of opportunity would miraculously work in her favour; that against the odds something might work out in time. In front of me was a Mum hoping for a future place for her son in a local specialist provision. We've had the meetings together and sent all the paperwork off in the correct timescales and are now just waiting on the panel's decision. The wait feels agonisingly long.

One of the most frustrating things to see over the years has been a lack of specialist placements for children with more complex and severe needs. We, like so many other mainstream settings around the country provide our very best within the resources that we have, but some children just need more. Over the years we have fostered close relationships with our local special schools. We've had dual placements for some children between both schools; they share their expertise with us, and we've joined with them for training and events such as interschool sports competitions. When you visit their settings, a number of things strike you. They not only have smaller class sizes and a greater flexibility of the curriculum, but they also have incredible resources . . . rooms fitted with what seems to be the latest technology, sensory areas and equipment that goes into the thousands of pounds, swimming pools and therapy centres and outdoor spaces that amaze. They're called special for a reason!

When there are not enough places like this for children who need them it's frustrating for us all. Perhaps hardest of all is when the powers that be agree that specialist provision is the most appropriate placement for a child but there are no spaces available, and so the child and the family have to wait until one appears . . . and because the spaces are like gold-dust they don't appear very often. The child and the family might have to wait a whole year down the line before things can finally slot into place, knowing that a different provision could provide their child with so much more, but having to wait for it. It's hard. Anxiety can increase for the family, and that can spill out in all sorts of ways. Our job is to work with them in the waiting. To keep giving them our best in the waiting. And today, this might be the case for this Mum sat with me. We've seen it before. The wait time is so tricky – everyone knowing that the current setting is not the best fit for the child but will somehow 'have to do'. That's never said out loud, but surely that must be how it feels for the family? 'Having to do' doesn't seem a good phrase to use when everyone wants what's best for the child. Surely that might feel a bit like they're getting second best? When these situations happen and we're all in this waiting game, we work so hard to provide what the child and family need, but it feels like there has to be a better solution.

At the end of the day, we have to know the systems within which we work. We have to have the information at our fingertips. We have to be informed. I don't like conversations with parents where you hold the tiniest bit of hope in one hand, and a good dose of reality in the other, knowing deep inside that it would feel like a miracle for everything to come together in time. But today it feels like it's been one of those conversations.

Be informed

*****

 REFLECT:

What emotions do you experience when you feel like you just have to 'make do' with a situation?

How do these feelings spill over into other areas or other relationships?

Is there someone you can come alongside in their waiting today?

26th September

Surprise!

That piece of paperwork I've been working on that I thought was needed for next week, now suddenly needs to be ready for tomorrow, because the person who wants to see it is now coming in earlier than expected. It's a surprise I could do without.

In school we use visual timetables to help children make sense of their day and create a sense of consistency and routine. We sometimes use a '?' card to represent a 'Surprise', for children who can find elements of uncertainty and changes to routine difficult. We use the card to try to help children understand that surprises can sometimes be fun even though they might have been unexpected, like Nanny popping in for a surprise visit, or an unplanned visit to the park, or going outside to sit under the shade of a tree for a story on a hot summer's day. The whole idea is to build children's resilience and support them amidst the change.

That said, sometimes life throws individuals or whole communities a pretty big 'surprise' card which has nothing fun about it for anyone. A problem that no one can see past. Maybe an accident that has an immediate impact or an illness with a looming prospect that hangs over someone for days, weeks or months, with no way of really knowing what is to come, how long it will last or what comes after. We all recognise that sick feeling we can get when we face an unwanted surprise that is thrown upon us. It's just often these feelings pass for us after the moment of stress has gone, and then we move on to a moment of relative ease.

The truth is that some of our children feel something daunting like this every day. Every day that knot of anxiety. What if some of the children in our schools feel this more regularly than we think? What if some of them feel an intense physical and emotional response daily, to lesser or greater degrees, without us even realising? It's a sobering thought.

**Be someone who sits with
your feelings, to use them for good**

*****

REFLECT:

What surprises could you have done without these past few weeks . . . and how did they make you feel?

Which children come to mind that need extra support around navigating what comes next?

What if you think past these known children to others you might not have identified yet?

27th September

I spent some time with Lucas this morning. He's been accessing a room with a few other children for a particular intervention every day, and he's been consistently more settled with this provision in place. By observing him, picking up on his non-verbal cues and talking with his mum, we're seeing the positive impact of the quieter environment on his levels of engagement and learning. Without the demands of numerous transitions throughout the day he's more at ease. With this time and space in a small group he's more settled both here and now, and afterwards. There's something about the quality of the interaction you can have with him in this time and space.

Quality interactions work. Giving children time and space to communicate, listen and learn, works. Lucas' settled-ness is not just down to preparation and planning. There's something about the space being all stripped back, all being scaled down. For children like Lucas, the sheer volume of people and places to navigate on a daily basis, and the complexity of a typical school day are barriers that can be overcome by tweaking the environment around him. But what if we dream bigger? What if we're not limited to considering the 'tweaks'? What if we were able to think about a radical overhaul of provision? What if school strategy and environments weren't limited by budgets? What if strategists, government and educational leaders had the luxury to create the provision that would enable all children to thrive? It feels like dreaming the impossible. But I guess I'm a dreamer.

Be a dreamer

*****

 REFLECT:

If money and resources were no object what would your provision look like?

What are your principles for supporting all children to thrive?

How do you sit with that tension of not having all you need?

25

28th September

We put so much time and effort into supporting children's emotional and mental health. It's a well-known premise that children have to feel safe and secure before they can be in a place where they're ready to learn. Because learning is a risky business. It's a place from which you experience something of not knowing before you then know. Where you experience something of not understanding before you then understand . . . and that's tricky. It's risky. You have to know that the diving board is safe and is going to take your weight before you can even consider walking along it, let alone jumping off when you get to the end. So we focus on emotional and mental health; on nurturing safe environments.

The problem is that we also have to focus on everything else at the same time, like the content of the curriculum in all its fullness . . . and the curriculum is full! There's lots to learn. Lots of amazing things and fun things, interesting and mind-boggling things, as well as boring things and things dreamt up by others who don't work in schools that we as professionals have no idea why they need to be taught at all. There's a pressure on everyone to squeeze it all in. Content and skills have to be covered, delivered and learned, and then you move onto the next thing. The problem is sometimes it doesn't feel like the balance is quite right. Sometimes children just need more time to learn the important things. Like being brave and trying again. Like, you're safe here.

And the other stuff can wait.

Be someone who knows what really matters

*****

REFLECT:

What do you think is the most important thing you teach your children?

If you could do away with certain parts of the curriculum, what would they be and why?

What do these things say about your values?

Monthly musings

September – A time of beginnings

Playgrounds full of nervous and excited children and parents anxious about how their children will settle or just relieved that it's the end of the long summer holidays. Colleagues fully prepped and ready to go, or starting hesitantly in new year groups or new to the job itself. Getting off to a good start is high on everyone's agenda. So, as we begin . . .

1 Reflect on what you want to bring to the children, families and colleagues you work with. What kind of person do you want them to know you to be? How do you communicate this?
2 Think about the contact or connection points you have with parents. Look out for parents who appear to be more isolated. Make sure you have a point of connection with each one. Make a point of catching their eye or getting in touch. If these connect points can't happen face to face, how can you work them into this month and then regularly going forwards?
3 Think about the language you use when you interact with parents, either face to face or in written form. It conveys so much. Avoid jargon, don't make assumptions and recognise that parents know their children best. Remember the importance of co-working and co-production with parents. It's about working together to best meet children's needs. Consider using your first name when you work with parents to support approachability. It can break down potential barriers for some families.
4 Reflect on the culture you want to build. What does that look like for you and your colleagues on a daily basis? Think about how you communicate this to children and parents or carers. If you have new colleagues starting in your setting, how do you communicate these things right from the start?
5 Put in the work to help new children and families settle. People are generally aware of how anxious parents may be in these

first few weeks, but also look beyond to how you can continue to build relationships throughout the year. Be quick to support and respond to settling-in issues, with both parents and colleagues. The speed with which you respond communicates a lot about value.

6 Is there a new practical skill or something you've been wanting to learn? Why not begin something and show the children what you're starting to learn. Share your progress with them throughout the year as you go along, to help them learn about effort, risk-taking, learning and resilience.

7 Broadly plan the year ahead. Look over your action plans and prioritise your next steps. Convey the heart behind your plans. Why are you aiming for the things you are? Cast the vision.

8 Identify training needs for colleagues. Ensure professional development is an ongoing priority to develop and consolidate your whole school expertise in meeting the needs of children with additional needs and SEND. Foster a culture of sharing skills and knowledge, of coaching and support. We're in this together.

9 Check that resources for individuals are in place and being used effectively. It develops trust if everything is ready from the outset and you're doing the things you said you were going to do in all your transition planning.

10 Encourage your colleagues. Communicate your thanks explicitly rather than hoping they just pick it up along the way.

NOTES – My musings . . .

September

📅 October

1st October

3.02am – Don't forget to email the Educational Psychologist to give them an update on all the ins and outs of this week in preparation for tomorrow's meeting.

3.08am – Don't forget to ask Cleo's class teacher to catch Mum first thing and remind her about the meeting tomorrow . . . because although she knows about the meeting, there's a chance that in the busy-ness of her week she might forget.

4.10am – Double-check that the room is still free, and that Mrs H has remembered she's covering your playground duty in case the meeting runs over.

5.35am – And still my brain won't shut off. Now I'm just thinking through all manner of different scenarios that could take place tomorrow at the meeting.

It's a good thing to know the parents we work with. To know their preferred methods of communication. To know what works for them, so that a good working relationship can be fostered. And even if our brain is whirring elsewhere . . . we need to be present in the moment. Not just present in the same physical space – but emotionally present. When we know we've got another meeting coming up, and that's the one that's taking up all our brain space (and has been taking up our head space for the last week, because we know it's potentially going to be tricky), we've still got to be emotionally present to the parent in front of us . . . the one we're talking with right now. Every parent needs to know that we're listening – really listening to what they are saying.

Be present

*****

DOI: 10.4324/9781003333753-3

31

REFLECT:

How easy do you find it do be 'present' with the person in front of you when your head is busy with other things?

How do you feel when you think the person you're talking to is not really listening or would rather be somewhere else?

2nd October

This morning I met with a parent who's considering their child coming to our school. She came armed with a file full of documents and reports from other professionals, as if she needed evidence to support her case. She wanted us to believe everything she said, everything she saw, everything she lived, because the behaviour she sees only happens at home, and it's not been observed at the child's preschool. So, she came prepared . . . as if before a judge in a court case. Prosecution and defence . . . My job was to listen, and think and listen.

With other prospective parents, you can sometimes physically see their hesitancy when they talk about their child. They're meeting with you because they want to know that you'll provide what their child needs – but in trying to find out if it's the right place of them, parents have to openly say what additional needs their child has, and for some, as they begin to speak, you can almost see them say 'Brace' when looking for our response. I have lost count of the number of prospective parents who have voiced less than positive experiences when they visit different schools. I've heard stories of Senior Leaders and Headteachers who have physically taken a step back when parents mention that their child is on the Autistic Spectrum when they're visiting a school. I've heard of schools where it would 'just be too difficult to . . .' whatever it is, without even being prepared to try.

And then I've seen parents breathe a sigh of relief when we're not concerned by the fact that their child is still in nappies, or that they have no verbal language . . . I love the inclusive ethos of our school. I love it that children don't bat an eyelid when they see a gastrostomy peg fitting when they're getting changed for PE. I love it that they sign to each other and hold the door open for their friend coming through in their wheelchair. I love it that they know that cochlear implants help children to hear. I love it that they know what fiddle toys and visual timetables and worry monsters are. I think our children and our whole school community are the better for it.

Be a culture builder

*****

REFLECT:

How do you welcome others?

When families approach you what are you good at, and what might you need to work on?

How do you build culture in your school?

3rd October

I know the whole OFSTED (government inspection) thing is not supposed to impact on your daily practice. Knowing that you're due an inspection shouldn't put pressure on you in the day to day, because they're just looking at what you already do, at what provision is already in place. That's what they say anyway. . . . As long as you know your children well and know what you do and why you do it; as long as you know how well you do it, the impact it has; as long as you know what needs to be improved or developed etc etc. . . . But in reality, it's not really like that. The truth is, knowing that they're coming someday soon does create pressure, no matter how well disguised it is, and it impacts on us all. Timeframes get shortened, ambitions get heightened, emotions get frayed. You get to the point when you just want it over and done with, like when you're sitting in the waiting room waiting for the dentist to call you in, knowing that he's going to be examining all your daily routines and care and letting you know if it's up to scratch.

When it comes to examining provision and outcomes for children with additional needs or SEND, this comes under particular scrutiny in an inspection, and rightly so. It just means as a SENCO, with the role of coordinating SEND provision within school, there's a weight upon your shoulders. Everyone makes it happen, but you have to guide it and lead it, along with rest of the senior leadership team. We're due an inspection in the coming year, or coming months, or coming days, and from time to time it kind of puts people on edge. I remind myself it's because we want to do well. We want people to see our dedication and hard work. We want the outcome to be a true reflection of where we're at, something that captures our heart, intention and capabilities as a school. What we don't want is a snapshot that somehow permanently records things a bit skew-whiff or off-centre or out of focus. We want people to understand the successes we celebrate, to see the progress that's been made and to recognise the community we create. The pressure might be mounting, but we're going to be ready.

Be ready

*****

REFLECT:

When your work comes under scrutiny what do you want people to see?

What do you want people to know about what you bring to the room?

What do you fear others might see?

5th October

We're encouraged to listen to parents. I mean really listen. And listen between the lines. There might be one thing they're talking about, but the *real* issue is something else entirely. . . . And we have this unwritten rule of, wherever possible, never having a conversation with a parent that could be tricky on a Friday – because come Monday, any anxiety or upset they have, may well have increased over the weekend, and then we could be dealing with a whole other ball game come Monday morning. This is what we do wherever possible . . . but today was a Friday.

Friday – 7.59am – Walk in through the door to be greeted by a colleague. 'Just to let you know that Mr W (parent) is cross with you' . . . . Ok, so that wasn't on my list of things to do today – but now it's a priority, and my to do list has suddenly shifted. Find out the facts and context. That means talking to Peter's teacher, the class LSA (Learning Support Assistant) and Midday Assistant before school starts, and then talk to Peter himself, and I need our Headteacher to be in the loop on this too and to agree a best plan of action. Remember Mr W's preferred method of communication – definitely face to face discussion, but not with other parents around – does he work on Tuesdays? – Check notes from before – Best number to call him on? Ask Peter's teacher to catch his dad at the start of the day to say I'll be in touch later this morning, so that he knows I'm responding, and so that he feels it's being done discretely. . . . Psyche myself up to make the call but keep it brief – just to arrange a proper meet-up tomorrow. Prepare. Celebrate what's working but note down key points we all want to discuss and be clear about. Don't skirt around the issue – We have a saying in our house about resolving conflict . . . there ain't no way through, but through. We're good at saying it but not always so good at doing it. I remind myself that we have to go through it, we can't manoeuvre round it or gloss over it, the only way through is through. . . . It calls for bravery, but it's never about barging in.

Be ready for a curve ball. . . . Everything inside me might feel that I need to form the 'brace' position . . . but listen. *Really* listen to what he has to say. Mr W needs to know that he's really been heard. That the offence he feels has happened has been taken seriously. That we're working together to problem-solve and move forwards. That's what person-centred planning is all about. Some parents so often feel that they are the last to know something; that they're only given part of the picture about their child, rather than the whole thing; that there are hidden agendas and that everyone else is keeping secrets behind their back. In the overall system, whilst liaising with any number of different providers and services, communication can very easily, accidentally, fall short of the best. It's something that can often be made better, and so we have to be intentional about good communication, because it's a foundation on which so much else is built. Make sure Mr W knows he's been heard, but more than that . . .

that you actually care. Not just because you want to cover your back, or look out for your colleagues, or protect the name of the school or avoid any further complaint – but ultimately because you actually care about Mr W's little boy, Peter, and that you want the best for him.

Be brave

*****

 REFLECT:

How do you respond to criticism?

What does being brave look like for you?

8th October

After nearly six weeks, little Adam walked through his classroom door this morning with a smile. It's been a long hard six weeks. His anxiety has often been overwhelming for him. Separating from his Mum and just getting through the classroom door has been a huge ordeal. His teacher was beaming when she walked into the staffroom at break. He did it! Let's shout it from the rooftops! One small step for him over the threshold, equals one giant leap for mankind. It's one of the things I love about my job. We all get to be a celebrator of small things – because for some, small things are momentously big.

Be a celebrator of small things

*****

 ## REFLECT:

What can you celebrate today?

Who could you tell?

What small thing is actually big for you?

9th October

To do lists. When it comes to supporting pupils and families with additional needs and SEN, everything on my list is a priority to someone. I might start the day knowing what I need to do, but one interaction can change it all – one phone call, one parent 'pop in' at the office can relay a paediatrician cancellation which means a child suddenly has an appointment on Monday – which means that report I'd been planning to write on Tuesday of next week now needs to be written today, so that parents and paediatrician get a copy of it in time. And we've learnt never to send a report out 'cold' to a parent, so that there are no surprises – we always talk them through it before. But if we're truly having person-centred dialogues, it should all be out in the open anyway. You've got to be so careful with your words, so that nothing can be misinterpreted. You only need to learn that the hard way once, to never want to do it again.

'To do' lists are a strange thing. They help with priorities, but they increase your stress if you only ever feel like you're adding to them, rather than crossing anything off. I think I should sometimes write 'go to the toilet' on my 'to do' list . . . just to fit it in somewhere in the day. To every parent, what they've just told you is a priority to them – they just might not realise that I have a whole host of other priorities that also need my attention ASAP. Every colleague wants your help today, and sometimes that 'today' is 'now!' Every professional you liaise with wants their strategies implemented, their resources in place straight away. People want every recommendation to be actioned today. And you want it too – because you want the best for every little person in your care. And for some, leaving something a day, is a day too late . . . a day when things have gone slightly 'wrong-er' than they were before.

It's a job full of spinning plates . . . juggling balls . . . jumping through hoops . . . tightrope-walking . . . fire-eating . . . and maybe some other kinds of Big Top analogies thrown in there too. You always feel like you're on the go, that you're swiftly moving from one thing to the next; that your next thing is waiting in the wings; that the programme is packed and there is no midway interval. You have to live with the tension that there are never enough hours in the day, and that you're not going to get everything done that you want to, or when you want to. But as a SENCO, as a teacher, as a member of support staff, as well as holding this 'to do list' tension, you're also navigating this amazing world of colour and light, pattern and life, every single day.

Be someone who can hold the tension

*****

 REFLECT:

What things are competing for your attention today?

How do you feel when you have to change your plans?

How does it feel to have to hold all these things in tension? . . . and who could you talk to about it?

10th October

Maybe another analogy of the SENCO role is that of a conductor of a musical piece. That's what I felt like today. At times the pace feels steady and even lyrical, but then with the turn of a page the score builds to a crescendo or finds itself frenzied with urgency. With baton in hand, you usher in this resource here and those over there, orchestrating provision and structure and melody and form so that things work together, so that the piece is complete. Very occasionally you finish the day with a pleasing sense of achievement . . . your work is done. You pause, and take a bow, waiting in silence, like the pause at the end of a piece before the audience stand to their feet to give their rapturous applause! This is a rare and wonderful thing! More often than not though, you finish the day somewhat sweaty and bedraggled, like the score got out of hand and you only just made it to the end in one piece. The thing about the job is you never know what piece of music you'll be playing on any given day. You can rehearse all you like, but life in school is like an everchanging musical score, with a life of its own. It's part of the joy as well as the strain.

Be an orchestrator of provision

*****

 REFLECT:

What kind of day is today? One where you're in control and the score is going to plan, or one where you feel more ragged?

If it's a bedraggled kind of a day, how could you take a few minutes to be kind to yourself?

11th October

A long time ago, in another school, I remember hearing about a newly appointed member of staff over lunch. She was in jovial mood, and yet was frustrated, talking about a child who had difficulty retaining things he had learnt from one day to the next. In a throw away comment she said she thought she should set up and invite the child to a craft club after school. She then proceeded to explain what kind of craft club she meant – 'Can't Remember A F . . . in Thing'. I remember feeling outraged. There are so many reasons why a child might not be able to retain information. Children with memory difficulties and language processing difficulties often struggle and try to mask their difficulties by copying behaviours that look like they're coping. Children who don't have their basic needs met might just be a bit more concerned about what's going on at home than what's going on in school. There are any number of reasons why they can't remember. It's our job to unpick the 'whys' and do something about it. It's not something to be ridiculed. The culture of a school is revealed and formed by the mini conversations that happen across any given day. Don't give unwelcome statements air. Don't let them breathe. Don't let them contaminate the air around you. Always speak highly of children. Always provide balance to skewed arguments. Always challenge and aspire to higher things.

Be a leader

*****

REFLECT:

How could you lead someone to make a better choice today?

How can you help others develop inclusive language and attitudes?

12th October

This morning I spent a good while with Robert who was struggling to come in through the door. I'm not even sure how we eventually managed to coax him out of the car, but I found myself trying to unpick what was going on for him. We've seen his anxiety before, but today it was off the scale. He was completely debilitated by his feelings . . . until a good 40 minutes down the line he suddenly hit a eureka moment. He was actually *good* at something. Actually, *really* good at something. He was far better at doing it than me (me being a full-grown adult, and him a six-year-old). He was the expert, instead of the failure he had as a recurring internal monologue . . . and it all started with talking about our holidays.

I'm willing to put my mind to most things, but there are two things I *cannot* do. (Yes, I know that's not the kind of language to be using when you think about having a growth mindset, but that's the point). . . . There are two things. Well, there are of course far more things, but for now I just want to consider two:

1 – Ski
2 – Crochet

I've tried skiing a couple of times. My first attempts were lessons when I was 46 years old, and then again two years later. I'd thought I was quite brave just giving it a go so late in the day, but where I'd hoped I'd see some small signs of improvement the second time round, things only got worse. My fear increased to the point that i) I physically could not control the shaking in my legs, and ii) my legs just locked in some kind of paralysis so that I literally couldn't change their position. Each day I got kitted up in the hope that things would improve, trying to stem the fear that was rising in my body, hoping I'd begin to feel even a tiny sense of control over my limbs, but to no avail. I realised that for me, maybe this wasn't the fun thing it was cracked up to be. Yes, I'd known it would be hard work, and that things wouldn't just fall into place overnight, but I'd hoped there'd be a glimmer of progress, just to keep me keeping on. On that second holiday, there were several occasions where I woke in the middle of night sobbing, my body heaving with all the pent-up frustrations of the day. And that's when I decided this wasn't fun, and I couldn't ski and probably that I wouldn't ski again.

Crocheting was far less traumatic. It consisted of watching a few tutorials online, watching a few friends and then a good friend modelling the basics close up, almost hand over hand, encouraging me to have a go. I can crochet a simple chain, but anything more complicated seems beyond my reach . . . but not to the point of tears. I could definitely give it another go, a concerted effort to push through the mental barrier. My friend recently crocheted this gorgeous deep green and blue throw, that inspired me to try again. . . . No immediate success, but whenever I see something beautifully made, I'll pick it up again and have another bash.

I'm ok with not being able to do these two things . . . because I don't come across the need to ski or crochet very often – they're life-skills I can do without, even though in my head I'd love to be able to master a crochet masterpiece, or whizz through powder on the Swiss Alps. But what if your fear of 'I just can't' . . . is just about stepping through the classroom door?

So there we were, talking about our holidays . . . and Robert suddenly realised that he was actually a brilliant skier, confidently mastering black runs with his family, whilst I shared my story of crying and shaky legs and that feeling of being frozen to the spot when I even put the skis on my feet . . . and the sharing of our two experiences, started to open up an inner self-belief for him on the one hand, as well as a safe place for him to begin to express how he felt about the process of writing . . . just putting pen to paper. . . . My vulnerability helped uncover his own . . . his feelings of being overwhelmed, of not knowing how to even start and feeling frozen to the spot, all came out into the open. . . . And that's some of why he had been literally frozen to the spot this morning. I knew what those physical feelings felt like, the aches were still in my legs, mine was just with a different trigger . . . and the sharing of vulnerability was like holding something precious, like treasure.

As SENCOs, it's part of our job to try and work out what's going on for children, to try to identify the internal and external barriers that get in the way of their learning. If we can tap into personal experiences where we hit barriers too, it reminds us of how big any accompanying emotions can feel. We are called, along with our teaching and support staff colleagues, to build trusting relationships with pupils, and within them, to forage, and to dig deep. For as we dig deep, we'll often find hidden gold that can be refined and polished so that it shines in ways we never imagined.

Be a goldminer and a keeper of treasure

*****

REFLECT:

What's something you find really difficult? How do you feel when you're trying to do it?

What do you feel emotionally and physically at the time?

How can that help you to empathise with others?

14th October

I was in a meeting today and I just couldn't read the room. Something just didn't sit right. I couldn't work out if there were some hidden dynamics I didn't know about, or if something else was going on, but I left with a feeling of uncertainty and lots of questions. Sometimes interactions with people can feel a bit unclear, like you're somehow doing that dodgy pavement walk of guessing which way the person coming towards you is going to walk. We kind of cue up the incoming on our approach and adjust our paths, like some awkward dance where both parties feel a bit out of synch, and no one really knows the moves.

I had a conversation today with one of our children who struggles with reading social cues at the best of times, and I can't help

47

wondering if the awkwardness we sometimes feel about what we do or don't do, can or can't do, should or shouldn't do, might just be a glimpse of what he faces every single day, where he has to interpret what's going on around him and try to make sense of social norms and practices that don't come naturally to him and many of us just take for granted. Sometimes we all need things spelling out a bit more explicitly. This is what's happening in this moment right here, right now. This is what's happening for you, and this is what's happening for me. When there's a lack of clarity about what's going on, when it feels vague and confusing, the feeling of awkwardness, the discomfort and the questions can help us empathise more with children who experience this each day.

Be an asker of questions

*****

 REFLECT:

Can you recall a situation where you couldn't read the room? How did it make you feel?

Which children come to mind that have difficulty picking up on social cues?

Are there ways in which you can support them more effectively?

15th October

6.45am Everything in me says I shouldn't be writing this. . . . It goes against everything I believe in and stand for . . . but please let Callum not be in today . . . just today . . . just to give everyone a bit of breathing space. Just to catch our breath so we can rethink. So we can come up with some other sort of plan. So we can recharge our batteries and be good to go again.

The problem isn't with Callum. It's with us. It's not really about his behaviour. It's about our current feelings of inadequacy to help him. At times we feel we don't know what to do. That's what's so debilitating. That's why we just need a breather. If there was just a simple formula you could learn and administer to gain breakthrough around supporting children to regulate their behaviour it would be simple, but things are more complicated than that. We're all complex. Of course, we know principles that help. We seek to be therapeutic in approach, to be informed about trauma and how best to respond; we have an understanding of attachment and know how the key is found in nurturing secure relationships, of creating consistent responses on our part with clear boundaries and supporting the child to co-regulate before they can move towards self-regulating their emotions; we understand about ACE's (Adverse Childhood Experiences) and their impact on children and society. We know the language and the theory; we know these are all key things to bring to the problem-solving process, but it's the actual practice of what to do in any given situation that gives you the confidence going forwards. What we really want is to feel totally skilled up, totally confident with what we need to do in the moment, every single time, in order to get it right.

But the truth is, you don't get to practise or become experienced on 'pretend' children. The only way we get to sharpen these tools is in the doing of them, with real children in real situations, and whilst we want to get it right every time, (because we want to get it right for the child), there will inevitably be times when we don't, and that doesn't sit well with any of us. Yes, we constantly reflect on our practice and learn from our mistakes, but it's not just us they affect. As a staff, when we're having training or when we're shadowing more experienced staff or being coached 'in the moment', we observe, we talk, we learn alongside. We study every subtle nuance of language and body gesture in the expert so that we build up our own quiet confidence of what to do on our own – but sometimes you don't just want to shadow or be coached through something, you kind of want to get inside the body and mind of someone who really knows what they're doing so that you can rehearse the moves, gain the quiet confidence and get the muscle memory before you have to do it on your own.

It can feel like you just want to keep your L-plates on a bit longer, that you're not fully qualified yet, but somehow, you've found yourself having passed your test and out on the road before you're ready. I remember an occasion when I was in my early twenties living in London. It was just before my driving test, and I was out with my instructor and the scene I remember vividly is sitting in the middle of a busy junction ready to turn right, when I stalled. Because we were so close to taking my test, my instructor just tucked his head down between his knees and said, 'Pippa, you get out of it'. My heart was racing, I felt sick; I wanted my instructor to talk me through what to do one more time, but however uncomfortable I felt, I had to do it on my own. Doing it on my own was the only way I was going to learn what to do in that situation if it happened again. I can recall the discomfort I felt even now.

8.51am Callum is in today – and everyone knows it. He doesn't want to be here either.

Be someone who pushes through the discomfort

*****

REFLECT:

What do you currently feel out of your depth with?
What could you do to take the next step in pushing through the discomfort?

16th October

I didn't get great sleep last night. As soon as my head hit the pillow I was out like a light, and that's usually how it works because I'm just so tired. But then I often wake in the night. Last night it was from about 2.30am until 4am just with stuff going through my head about the different things and challenges I knew I had ahead of me today. I walked into the staffroom first thing to be greeted by a colleague saying, 'You look fresh this morning!', to which I replied, 'It's amazing what a quick wash of the hair and bit of eyeliner can do', but really I wasn't feeling fresh at all.

And then I touched base with a parent who knows what real sleep deprivation looks like. Day in, day out – or rather, night in, night out. We should take our hats off to these people and cheer them on from the side-lines. Some children with additional needs just don't seem wired to sleep for long periods of time. Some take most of the evening into the early hours just to settle, and others settle but then wake any time from 4am, and then both they and their parents feel like they've done a day's work before they even get to school. Sometimes we just need to get some perspective and appreciate the things we might well be taking for granted. So, I'm still tired, but now the weight of it just feels a bit different.

Be appreciative

*****

 REFLECT:

What could you be appreciative of today?

Who could you talk to to give you a different perspective about something?

17th October

The past couple of days has included some conversations with parents about provision going forwards. What's going to be the best for their child as they think about their next school placement? Honest, hard, sensitive two-way conversations.

But conversations are made easier if you have good relationships with your parents. Because then, conversations are borne out of and built on the trust you've grown together over the years, where parents know that you really do want the best for their children and them as a family. There's that game of trust that you sometimes play as a child, where one person shuts their eyes, plants their feet and lets themselves fall back, trusting that a partner will catch them. This is what these kinds of conversations can look like and feel like. We have to recognise the risk involved as we embark on these and we have to let parents know we've got our hands out ready to catch.

Be a trust-builder

*****

 REFLECT:

How do you build trust with the parents you work with?

How do you feel when you anticipate potentially tricky conversations?

How can you best prepare for them?

19th October

I wish we could just crack him. . . . That's what I've been thinking. Not crack as in break, but crack as in crack the code or get through the hardened exterior and crack open the treasure inside.

Supporting children with social, emotional and mental health needs is really rewarding, but is also really challenging, and it's long, hard work. The whole school can feel affected by the presence of just one child, and we're all really feeling it at the moment. Supporting each other and teamwork kicks in, but it's ok to sometimes feel out of your depth. I know not all schools share the same ethos. Every school needs to create a culture where it's ok to ask for help, without fear of any sense of shame. We need to foster the ethos that we're all in this together. But there's the rub. Because sometimes in schools, if we're not careful, it can feel like we're just looking after ourselves. Not because we necessarily want to, but because we're so focused on what we have to achieve. There's such a pressure in the system for teachers to reach targets set for each of their children; to evidence the progress each child has made. If you're not careful, a 'look after yourself' mentality can set in. When you're under pressure, you tend to batten down the hatches and just keep going, and that can make asking for help or offering help difficult. We're only supposed to show progress, to hit and exceed targets and so the pressure is always on . . . and it's all the more complex because somehow, somewhere along the way, staff meeting targets became inextricably linked to performance and pay and capability.

We need to build team at every opportunity . . . and we need to recognise that when supporting children with extremely complex needs, the demands are often high. Sadly, the challenges of supporting some pupils, often with insufficient resources, support or training, can leave people feeling isolated, vulnerable and depleted of resources. In schools, our job is to cultivate a supportive team, to inspire, as well as be real with the challenges we face.

Be aware of the challenges

*****

REFLECT:

What challenges are you currently facing?

Who can you ask for support along the way?

What kind of support do you feel you need?

22nd October

There are some children who, for a whole variety of reasons, live in a regular state of unsettled-ness. Where normal day to day living is a lack of calm, and the perpetual nature of unease has this exponential impact over time. I was thinking about one of our little ones with whom we continually seek to build and rebuild foundations of relationship and security.

In my mind's eye I have this image of shingle on a beach, and a huge storm-wave comes in churning up all the water, and pebbles and stones get thrown around, tossed up and down, and bashed around by the conflicting currents and movement of the water. Churned up.

I wonder if this is what he's feeling? Like there's no settling; no stability; like he can't see or feel firm ground; like he doesn't know which way is up or down; like he's unsure when another wave might come and sweep him off his feet. When you're tossed around, you have to allow yourself to settle, you have to trust the process, the downward pull of gravity that will settle you in time on the surface below. But what if you've tried to allow that before, and just as you begin to land on the seabed everything just gets churned up again? Each cycle of re-settling surely takes longer, because the uncertainty feels greater, and he can't actually remember what it feels like to be calm and settled, he doesn't actually know what that feels like at all. It's going to be a while before he feels at ease. Before he feels safe.

Be someone who helps others to ride out the storm

*****

 REFLECT:

How do you feel when you don't feel safe?

How do you support children who feel like this on a daily basis?

How do you as a school build a sense of safety?

23rd October

Over the years I've taken to getting everything ready for work the night before or sometimes making a list so that I don't forget something vital. This morning I'd done a last-minute change of my jacket, and it wasn't until I parked my car when I got to school that I realised I'd left my key entry fob in the pocket of my other coat. There was no doubt I'd be let in, it's just I knew someone might not be in the office straight away, and it could cause a bit of inconvenience to someone else as well as me. So, whilst the mini sense of panic soon subsided, what I felt in that moment was that feeling of having forgotten something, that feeling of being momentarily disorientated, of frustration and stupidity.

Some children we work with struggle with organising their belongings and getting ready what they need for the day. We give them tools to help remember things, whether it be a visual checklist, an object as a physical reminder, a mnemonic or song, a peer to prompt and all the time we seek to build their independence. If we can remember what it can feel like when it goes a bit wrong for us, we can empathise with children when they feel something similar. Maybe they've only forgotten something small; maybe they've forgotten something that seems irrelevant to us but might be of huge importance to them; maybe they've forgotten something crucial. Maybe they forget things and feel that sense of disorientation day after day. We have to feel the feelings. Sometimes they pass and sometimes they linger on into the rest of the day. So, note to self . . . to remember the feeling, but next time to also remember to check my list.

Be alert to your feelings

*****

REFLECT:

How do you feel when you forget something? Does the feeling pass or stay with you for a while? Does it depend on where and when it happens and who you're with at the time?

Imagine experiencing that feeling again and again, anticipating it and dreading it at the same time. . . . How can you support children who may feel like this regularly?

24th October

I was with one of our parent governors today and she recounted a story of her son talking about his day at school and a conversation he'd had with his friends. The story went something like this . . . 'and she said 'Oh' and he said, 'Yes' and he said '. . . .' (and he made a squeal). It was all just so matter of fact. In his retelling of what had happened, he had shared his peers' responses, some of them verbal and one in the form of a vocalisation. There were no articulated words from this particular child who is predominantly non-verbal in his communication, but to the child retelling the story, he was just one of the people present and was included in the recount without the bat of an eyelid. The mum said that's what she loved about our school.

Be inclusive

*****

 REFLECT:

What are the children in your school learning about diversity and inclusion just by being a part of your school community?

What about if you asked the same question of your parents?

What do you love about inclusion?

25th October

'Choose me, choose me!' Anyone who's been in a classroom of five- or six-year-olds will know the eager waggle of the hand in the air, the wriggle of the bottom trying to edge them higher to stand out from the splatter of other outstretched arms. There's an eagerness to share their idea or give an answer that they hope will leave them with that glowing feeling of being right or being seen or being proud.

And there's those who so desperately want to be chosen, to be seen, to be noticed, that they try to get your attention in all sorts of ways, where everything about what they say and do says 'notice me!', even if what they're doing is not what you want to see at all. And so there's this cry for connection, this plea for relationship, and we engage in this balancing act of affirming and noticing and choosing the child, because that's what they so need, but not in this particular moment for this particular behaviour.

There's those who are tentative in their response, who bravely offer their 'choose me' by giving it a go, wanting and yet not wanting to put themselves on the line. Sometimes it's a very brave thing to put your hand in the air just in case you're noticed.

Then there's those who don't want to be noticed at all. Those who want to shrink away or be passed over, those who hope to God you won't single them out or choose them for fear they'll not know something they feel they should know.

And our job is to know all these children and all the kinds of children in between. Our job is to know these things, so that we can gently ease those who want to remain unseen into a careful (care-full, full of care) place of being seen and feeling safe in the seeing, so that we can build trust with those who fear rejection, so that we can celebrate the sheer grit of the child who has persisted until they've got that breakthrough of understanding, so that we can nurture an awareness of others in one by not choosing them in the moment but choosing another, and helping them note the joy on that face.

When it comes to choosing, we must choose carefully. We must notice and see and be alert in all kinds of ways.

Be a seer

*****

REFLECT:

Do you like being chosen or put in the spotlight? Why?

Who are the children who stand out and it's easy to see? What do they need?

Who are the children who want to stay hidden? What do they need?

Monthly musings

October – Building trust

Some children will be settling well, whereas others may need longer to feel comfortable in their new surroundings. The same goes for parents and wider families. So we keep on intentionally building relationships, recognising that this is setting foundations for the rest of the year and the years to come . . .

1 Reflect on how children and families are settling. Are there some you need to focus on more than others at this time? Get to know the ways different parents prefer to communicate with you – face to face, in the playground, at the door, via email, phone or video call. Make a mental note to use their preferred method wherever possible.

2 Continue to do the work of identifying children's barriers to learning. Which of these are barriers internal to the child that you need to explore further, and which might be external barriers that you can decrease or eliminate with alterations to the environment? Remember that environment might also be you!

3 Think about a parent who might be anxious about receiving a call from school in case it is about something that is not going so well. Can you start to change this sense of anticipation by calling and encouraging them with something about their child?

4 Examine any current frustrations. Which of them are smaller and perhaps more easily remedied, and which are bigger challenges that may require more in-depth solutions over time? Identify a next step for each that might make a difference.

5 Start the habit of noting down things that encourage you each week, whether that be an interaction or breakthrough with a child or parent, or a word of encouragement from a colleague. Don't just look for the big things, notice the small too. If you can't think of any, ask a colleague to help. Sometimes we just need another pair of eyes to notice something in the middle of all the busy.

6   Consider how you can build moments of rest or relaxation into your regular week. What might that look like for you? Be intentional about making this happen.

7   With some children, the honeymoon period may well now be over. As children begin to feel safer in their new surroundings you may begin to see new behaviours. Where some may have been putting considerable effort into masking their needs or containing their reactions, things may now start to spill out either in school or at home. Reassure parents who may be disconcerted by this. Work together to adapt provision and find solutions. If children are releasing their pent-up emotions or reactions at home, it's important that parents know to communicate this to you. Wherever it's happening, the behaviour is communicating some kind of unmet need. What might these things be highlighting or communicating?

8   Think about the current support structures you have in place as a staff. How effective are they for you and your colleagues? Strategy and structures that may have worked well in the past may need tweaking in the context of your current staff team. Where might there need to be changes? Discuss what might be helpful together.

9   Continue to build relationships with parents. Remember, with every interaction you will be communicating so much about how you welcome children and families.

10   Check the consistency of language and positive approach used amongst all of you as a staff team around SEND. Is the ethos you're seeking to communicate being reiterated by all your colleagues or is there any mixed messaging?

NOTES – My musings . . .

November

8th November

People sometimes come to you and just want you to wave a magic wand. To disappear things away with a puff of smoke. Don't fall into the trap. There is no magic wand. You are not a one man/woman superhero. If you try to be, you will wear yourself into the ground within a few weeks. Journeying with people, whether it is fellow colleagues, parents or children, is often more about hard graft – the daily effort of turning up, of being present, of problem-solving, of planning and reviewing how things are going, of tweaking things here or there and in some cases radically overhauling practice. It's about passion and commitment from us all, and at the heart of it, an intention to work together to provide the best we possibly can for each child. It's a team effort, partnering with everyone involved, through thick and thin. Lots of the children we work with have long term needs, and if there were easy answers, someone would have come up with them by now. People are complex. Each with a unique set of strengths, needs, history, personalities and characters.

The flip side of disappearing something away, is people wanting you to wave your magic wand and pooooofff!!! . . . something will *appear*. Something coming out of nothing. Da dah!!!!. . . . Maybe conjuring up a new member of staff to support a child, or fast-tracking years of experience into just a day so that someone feels ready and equipped for the task, or magic-ing money out of nowhere for resources. . . . But it doesn't work like that either. We have an imaginary member of staff in our school. It arose in my early days of working here. I was trying to recall the name of a member of staff in my first week, in a sea of new faces, and inadvertently referred to someone by referring to the first name of one person and a slightly mis-recalled surname of another – hence an entirely new person. My attempt was met with confusion and then laughter as my mistake came to light, but this fictional person's name lives on. She's the person we always turn to when we need to find someone to fit

DOI: 10.4324/9781003333753-4

65

the bill. The problem is she's not real. She doesn't actually appear when we need her. Waving your magic wand doesn't work. So, don't be a fairy godmother, but do be a hope-bearer. Cast vision. In the hard graft, be someone who says keep going, let's do this together and seek for something more, something better. Let's be people who gather scattered hope as we work together.

Be a hope-bearer

*****

 REFLECT:

If you could wish something away right now, what would it be?

Or if you could make something magically appear, what would it be?

Who could you ask to help gather scattered hope together, and what might that look like?

9th November

'Do you know what I love most?' . . . Pause . . . 'Stones', he said. This caught me a bit off guard. Because up until this point it had been something else entirely for the whole time I've known this young man. But now, the thing he loves most is stones, and this is important to him and so needs to be known by us. We put in hours of work with children, parents and families so that we can together gain a detailed and broad understanding of them as a person . . . not just their needs . . . but them, their whole little selves . . . the fact that they love sitting upside down on the sofa while they're watching TV . . . that they know more about planets and galaxies than I'll ever know, and the fact that their favourite thing now is collecting stones. . . . It's all to do with being person-centred. Our challenge is always how to keep being person-centred when sometimes it doesn't feel like the system sees the person.

Be a collector of detail

*****

 REFLECT:

How do you feel when someone makes assumptions or doesn't know all the correct details about you?

Think of a child. What more details might you or others need to know to help support them better?

Do you feel 'seen' and that others know all the details when it comes to meeting the needs of this child? If not, who could you talk to about this?

12th November

One of the best things we've ever done is set up a Parent Coffee Morning to support parents of children with SEND and additional needs. I'm not boasting. I genuinely think it is one of the best things we've done. It happens once a month, and it's a place where parents come along, and over a cup of tea and some biscuits, get to hang out. Sometimes we just sit and chat, sometimes we focus on specific topics of discussion, sometimes we problem-solve, sometimes we do training, whether that be internally or with outside speakers coming in. It's a place where parents can come and feel like they're not on their own; where they know that others might share a similar story; where they can be supported so they feel like they're not going mad; where they can say how things are going for them and feel the safety of not being judged; where they can share ideas and pick up hints about what's available locally to support them as families (whether that be finding out about a hairdresser who's brilliant at supporting children who find haircuts excruciatingly uncomfortable due to their sensory needs, or where a local swimming instructor takes the time to help children get into the water and offers individual support to children where it's needed, or whether it's a local Brownie pack where a member of the team signs BSL – British Sign Language). Yes, you can search up local information about what's out there, but word of mouth is far more powerful, because it's tried and tested. Trusted. And that's what the group does. It builds relationships and it builds trust.

Sometimes I feel like my diary is too full to make it happen. Sometimes we have lots of parents, sometimes just a few, but pretty much every time, it feels life-giving. Investing in and creating space for building parent-staff relationships is never a waste of time. You always reap what you sow. . . . and what's wonderful is hearing the connections parents then make with each other outside of the group . . . the wave across the playground, the encouraging nod or offer of help when one of them is having a pear-shaped morning. Today's session was a highlight in my week, watching a parent who during her first year of attending was super hesitant, now coming out of her shell and offering advice from her own story and experience to other parents. Her quiet strength and newly voiced confidence were wonderful to see.

Be a creator of space

*****

REFLECT:

What space could you create to encourage people to share their stories?

What good ideas do you have and who could you share them with?

Where do you sometimes wonder if you have the time for something but know it's too valuable to miss?

13th November

So today I am sat in a review meeting with a parent I hardly know, with the Educational Psychologist, talking about serious things, dressed in my spotty pyjamas. It's coincided with a fancy-dress raising money for charity day. I don't know whether to feel awkward or just to say it out loud and embrace the moment. I go for the latter. All in a day's work and all that! But note to self, to always find out when it's happening and remember to write it in my diary first!

Be able to laugh at yourself

*****

REFLECT:

When was the last time you had a good laugh about yourself or with others?

What was it about?

What did it teach you about yourself?

14th November

I feel pulled in all directions. So many things being asked of me by different people. Everyone needing something today . . . I know I'm part of a hard-working team, but there's only one of me!

Sometimes being a SENCO can feel a bit of a lonely job, which is strange, because the role is so busy with people. But the weight of it can often weigh heavily on your shoulders. It's a role where the buck stops with you in lots of ways. Yes, there's a joint responsibility with the Senior Leadership Team and Head, and there are many things for which the Governing Body is ultimately responsible, but there are some things, some elements of the job, that others won't know about unless you tell them. The problem is the role is so vast, and other people only really tend to see just one part of the picture. The one part that they're involved in. That might be calling on you for support with planning for a child, or support around a child's behaviour, or collating and analysing data, or making strategic decisions about training and resources, or meeting with a distressed parent. The list is endless. It's one of the reasons I love the job, because it's so varied, and you can never tell how any given day is going to pan out. But it also comes with a level of stress.

I'm thankful I'm in a position where my SENCO role is non-class based and I haven't had to juggle teaching a class at the same time, but the reality is that for many of us in the job, we're wearing several hats all at the same time – whether that be as an additional Designated Safeguarding Lead or curriculum area lead, and in smaller schools, everything else thrown in. I know of some SENCOs who have minimal time to fulfil their SENCO role, often where non-teaching time is not protected, and staff are then drawn on to cover staff absence as well as other things. It makes a job which is already extensive in its remit nigh on impossible. The extent of the role has to be understood by Senior Leadership Team down, and then backed up with support, time and resources. Thank God I'm in a school where it's valued and seen as part of the foundations of the school. But even so, the pressure's always on to get everything done. Not everyone needs to know (because we're all incredibly busy in schools), but someone needs to know the fullness of the task and the times when it all feels a bit much.

Be a describer of the full picture

*****

REFLECT:

Is there someone who knows what your day really looks like today? Someone who sees all the 'busy' that you're trying to cram in, and the challenges that it includes?

If you feel unseen, could you describe the full picture to someone? And what would that look like?

17th November

I am short-sighted. My eyesight has deteriorated over the years to the extent that without my glasses on, pretty much everything that is not right in front of my eyes is blurry. Without anything to remedy the situation, it's all very disorientating. So, the first thing I do when I wake up is go to the bathroom and put my contact lenses in. This morning was an exception, because it's the weekend and I decided to have a leisurely start to the day. Big mug of tea in my pyjamas, glasses on . . . except they were smudgy, so I took them off, and then looked around, and everything was a blur. It's disconcerting being disorientated. Even though I'm in a familiar environment, there's still something unsettling about it, because I can't see clearly. In this moment, I can't see the expression on my daughter's face across the room; I can't see what that is on the floor in the corner, yet I know it's something that's not usually there; I can't see who that is walking past the window that's just dropped something through the letterbox.

Immediately I thought about an annual review meeting I had this week for a child with visual impairment. He has an EHCP (Education Health and Care Plan) with a high level of funding to support him. I remember reading his EHCP before I first met him, weeks before he arrived at our school, and the medical terminology felt like a bamboozling read, but we put in the work to try to understand what this meant for this little boy and how his visual impairment impacted on his daily life. At one point during our Annual Review discussion, I asked the child's Mum whether she thought her little boy would be able to tell us if he was finding things tricky to see. What I meant was, was he giving us the full picture, i.e. would he have the confidence to tell us if he couldn't see something and needed more help, or might that be difficult for him in some way. That's what I meant. But as soon as the words came out of my mouth, I realised my folly. 'He can only see what he can see' said the VI (Visual Impairment) Specialist Teacher. Ching! Light bulb moment. Of course! For someone like this child with his particular complexities of visual impairment, you can only see what you can see. You don't know what you can't see because you can't see it. It's like you don't know what you don't know . . . until you know it!

It's the same for us, and the same for all our colleagues. We may have a treasure trove of information, insight and knowledge about different areas of need and strategies that support different children, but it's no good that information just staying with us. Of course, much of our role is to share and develop expertise across the whole staff, so that we can meet the needs of all pupils. So, let's embrace every light bulb moment; let's model being learners and value new ways of seeing things. There's always more to learn, always more to see.

Be a learner

*****

REFLECT:

When was your last 'light bulb' moment? What did you learn?

What do you want to learn or find out more about over the next few weeks?

How will you go about doing that?

19th November

We're in full swing with Christmas rehearsals in school and the sound of children singing songs can be heard in the corridors. There's a buzz in the air and walking through the hall on the way to the library area a class is rehearsing and a moment catches my eye, so I linger a little longer than intended. The message I needed to give to someone can wait a while. I am the unplanned, impromptu audience, and Max is not only sat with the rest of his class, but when the right time comes, he gets up, and holding his friend's hand moves into the space in front of him and bangs his drum with all his might. He enjoys all things musical and loves to bang and crash things together, so being able to drum is a way he can participate with his friends doing something he loves. It's something that makes him happy. It's something he feels comfortable with . . .

There are things about school that are sometimes less comfortable for him. Things that increase his anxiety. Max struggles if something happens unexpectedly and there has been little prewarning or preparation, and he doesn't yet have the verbal language to express how he feels. He struggles with even small aspects of change, so getting to a place where he feels happy to be in the hall doing something different has been a long, planned process, using visuals and gradual exposure to new things one step at a time. Small steppingstones crossed along the way to help him face new experiences. Knowing him and planning to alleviate his anxiety is key – planning to support each transition, knowing what he loves, what helps, what calms, as well as what triggers discomfort or difficulties. Gaining his views by observing him closely and responding to his non-verbal communication; talking with his parents and people who know him well have helped to build the picture. The staff team around him have worked hard to support him to feel comfortable, and to support his increasing engagement in the activity over time. So, glimpsing him not only participating in it all, but also enjoying it is one of those moments that makes you want to sing! This is one of the things I love about this job. Things that might not even register with other onlookers . . . this seemingly small success that is actually a huge, giant thing to celebrate. This is the kind of achievement that not everyone measures, that some just take for granted and others just belittle. But for us it's the kind of success that puts a broad smile on your face and gives you a spring in your step. Others might not appreciate all the work that has gone into it, but we know it. Max and his family know it. We appreciate it and so do they. So, let's capture the moment, join the celebration and bang the drum!

Be a capturer of the moment

*****

REFLECT:

What recent moment do you want to capture about a child, and why?

Who might not see it in the same way as you, and could you find a way to tell them why it's so important to you?

22nd November

Today we're preparing for a child who's moving house and moving to a new school after the Christmas break. It's when you look back on your time with them that you begin to recall all the interactions you've had with them and their families. All the conversations. All the detailed knowledge they've shared with you, all the confidences you've kept. The privilege it's been.

When a child leaves school it's like you erase all trace of them. All paperwork and electronic records get passed on to their new school with consent, their books go with them and you erase them completely. But the thing is, you can't . . . and most of the time, you don't want to.

What you can't erase is the memories . . . the smile they had from ear to ear, the persistence they showed to just keep going, the way they gave you daily updates on their hamster, the pride they had showing off their new haircut, their cheeky quips, their sighs and frustrations when they found things difficult. The legal stuff might be passed on and gone from sight, but the child and family somehow stay with you.

Be confidential

*****

 REFLECT:

Think of a child you remember from a while back. What is it about them that you recall?

Why do you think this memory has stayed with you?

What did you learn about yourself when you worked with them?

23rd November

Walking back to my room, I could hear the sound of the piano being played in the corridor. I knew that meant that a specific member of staff was there, and that more than likely she would be accompanied by one of her pupils. She's good at improvising on the piano and improvising with this child. Not that there aren't careful, considered plans in place for him, but she's a skilled practitioner – good at thinking on her feet and responding in the moment. She knows that listening to music and participating in making music just does something for this child, so now it's written into his plan. It somehow soothes and settles him back to a state of calm if he's become emotionally heightened. It settles him to a place where they can then begin to explore what's happened and how to move forward. We're involved in so much planning around children with additional and special educational needs, but when you know them well, sometimes there's still cause to seize a moment and improvise . . . and then the improvise becomes part of the plan.

Be able to improvise

*****

REFLECT:

Do you feel that you have the freedom to improvise with some of the children in your care?

How do you hold the tension of planning and yet improvising?

Are there any children where you feel all run out of ideas? Who could you turn to for help to explore creative ideas or try to find solutions together?

Monthly musings

November – Health checkpoint

Coughs, colds and bugs are probably circulating well by now, and things will only start to get busier and more tiring over the next few weeks as everyone prepares for all sorts of celebrations. So now is a good time to check in with how everyone's doing, including yourself.

1 How do you keep well? How do you try to create some sort of work-life balance?
2 Consider how you're feeling. They're an important indicator of how you're doing, and an internal dialogue about your hopes and dreams, frustrations and disappointments. Press into life-giving relationships, both in and out of school.
3 Be real about anything you're struggling with. Don't moan but do get it out in the open with someone you trust. Problem-solve with others to explore solutions.
4 Reflect on why you do what you do. What is it about your job that you love?
5 Try to pace yourself. What are your priorities and why? What do these choices convey about your values?
6 How well are you able to assess and respond to your capacity in the moment?
7 Think about the support your colleagues have. Are there further ways in which you can develop effective and meaningful staff wellbeing?
8 What are some of the pressure points that you come across regularly? Are there things that can be put in place to alleviate some of these?
9 Audit your SEND paperwork. Ask your colleagues – is the paperwork around SEND being used in the way it was intended? Is it fulfilling its purpose? It is useful? Is it workable?

Is the information duplicated elsewhere? Are there processes you can streamline to make more efficient?

10 Consider the wellbeing of the children and parents you work with. What practices do you consistently have in place to support them? Are these practices working?

NOTES – My musings . . .

📅 December

3rd December

8.30am – Mrs L's off sick, and Mr F's just been sent home looking green . . . and we've got to find cover for Priya and Rory in the next 10 mins, and Ms B doesn't work on a Mon, and Miss A can't do it because her daughter's also off with the same lurgy . . . and we can't put so and so with Priya because it's not a good skills match, and Priya needs to have someone who's got the experience to meet her needs, and it's the Reception class Christmas assembly today!!!! If Miss D can do it, that means we'll need to get cover for Lily, and then Hamilton . . . so, we'll need to speak to Mrs S and Mr J.

8.38am – Miss D can do it! Thank goodness . . . because Mr F's gone home, I need to make sure Ms H goes through Lily's plan for the day, especially the new tweak in the plan about lunchtimes, and ensure that Mrs M checks in with Miss D so that she knows what she's doing.

11.38 – Miss D needs to have lunch!? We forgot lunch!! Mrs L's off sick, and Mr F's gone home, Ms B doesn't work on a Mon, and Miss A can't do it because her daughter's also off with the same lurgy. Between Mrs J and I, we'll do it . . . I'm supposed to be observing Mia on the playground, but I can observe Mia tomorrow. I'll grab lunch in car en-route to the SENCO Cluster meeting at 1pm.

Matching people to children's needs is not always as easy as it sounds. It's not like loosely pairing up plain socks as they come out of the dryer. Children's needs are complex, and you can't just allocate anybody with anybody. Children deserve expertise; they deserve that we work hard to match their support so that it's the best for them; that we consider personal dynamics and aim for consistency of routine and support wherever possible. We would want the same considerations to be made if we were in their shoes or pairing up our own socks. Our aim is always to develop children's independence so that children do not become reliant on people, and

DOI: 10.4324/9781003333753-5

to do that you have to build a rich, flexible, multi-skilled team of people who have the best interests of the children at heart.

Be flexible, and be part of the team

*****

 REFLECT:

How good are you at being flexible?

What helps to build confidence and flexibility within your staff teams?

4th December

Yeeesss!!! Kaelan said his three words in the Christmas play! We knew that he could. We just weren't sure if he would on the day itself. I love my job!!!! All the rehearsal, all the investment, all the practice paid off . . . and only we and his parents and Kaelan himself will ever really know all the little steps and all the effort, and all the bravery that led to that moment of triumph. And what a moment of triumph!

Be triumphant

*****

REFLECT:

Which children and families do you particularly feel invested in right now? Imagine what you might see in them in the future. What could it look like? How would that make you feel?

5th December

It's that time of year where school is filled with excited chatter, and whenever you walk past an open door you hear Christmas refrains being sung as children rehearse their words. We all love the collective festive gatherings in the hall with proud parents looking on as the wider school community celebrate together. But it's a busy, busy time, and there's a varying level of 'feeling shattered' amongst us all.

Today was Christmas Dinner Day. There were reindeer antlers, pudding hats and light-up Christmas jumpers. The festivities included singing and reading out cracker jokes whilst watching the sometimes slightly delayed joy of the punchline sinking in.

As I helped support a child to cut up their dinner, I heard another one pipe up, 'This is the best Christmas dinner ever!' . . . I asked her why, and her reply was 'because we've got crackers!', as she pulled one with a friend and hunted for the prize within. She didn't even notice the busyness of the season or the disguised tiredness on all our faces. She still managed to feel the excitement of those added extras that we always have on special occasions, but I'd just lost sight of them for a moment. She'd managed to find the joy in the rough. Young children can have this remarkable way of seeing things.

Be childlike

*****

 REFLECT:

Think of a child. What might be their perspective on your day today?

How do you think you sometimes see things differently to the children around you?

Can you spot a moment of joy that you'd previously overlooked?

7th December

We're all feeling a bit jittery. We've got a couple of weeks to go now until the end of term, and all of us are hoping and praying that we don't go down with something over the Christmas break. There's been a flu-ey thing going round and a vomiting thing going round, and none of us want it now or during the holidays. Sometimes it just feels like it always happens. No matter how hard you try you just end up going down with whatever 'it' is going round. Ben coughed and spluttered in my room today when he was showing me something he'd been working on, and although I was looking and listening intently, I also couldn't help but think about all the germs that were now floating about the air. So, I left my door open when he left, and quickly washed my hands when I got a chance.

When it comes to inclusion you have to be determined about a lot of things when you work in a school. Determined to keep on going when things get tough, determined to press into values you hold dear, determined to fight for people's causes, determined to advocate for those who feel they don't have a voice. Determination is a basic requirement . . . and this close to the end of term while we're making plans with our friends and families, amidst the general weariness, there's a collective determination in the air to not get sick!

Be determined

*****

REFLECT:

Think of someone you would consider to be determined. What is it that you admire about them?

What are you determined to do or be in school?

8th December

This morning I was talking to parents at our monthly drop-in café for parents of children with additional needs. We were talking about Christmas and how we can support children when routines change, as the potential for sensory overload increases over the festive season. The café provides a safe and supportive place for parents to connect and share ideas, and today reminded me why we do it, when a mum new to the group joined for the first time. She's someone we are journeying with as we unpick the underlying needs for her child, and at the end of the session she just said how she now really felt like she wasn't on her own, and that she knew there were others out there going through similar things each day. As parents drop off and collect their children at both ends of the day, some find it easier to connect and develop supporting relationships than others, so we need to keep creating and protecting safe spaces where this can happen.

Be a protector of safe space

*****

REFLECT:

How can you create a safe space for parents to connect in school?

What could it look like?

What might it achieve for individual parents and the whole school community?

11th December

It seemed like an easy question – 'How was your day?' as I walked through the door, flopped my bag on the floor and kicked my shoes off. But I didn't even know where to start. How was my day? It's something I love about the job, the unpredictability of it, the fact that you never know what's going to happen next, the fact that no one day is the same as another, but it's also something that keeps me on my toes, and sometimes my toes just feel tired of being kept on.

There's all the stuff scheduled in my diary on any given day, but it's also all the other stuff that happens. All the catching people for quick updates about different children; all the emotional ups and downs of the day; all the conversations to-ing and fro-ing; all the information you just carry in your head. I never knew how much information a brain could hold until I started this job. So, I just answered the question with a 'Busy'. I think you can only really 'get' how busy it is when you've worked in a school and experienced it for yourself, and any kind of trying to explain it to others can just feel frustrating because they won't really understand. So 'busy' would have to do for now, until I had the energy to try to expand on it.

Big thankyous for asking, but telling people who may not ever be able to really 'get it' sometimes feels worse than not telling them about it at all. But to all my friends and family, please do keep asking, because at some point, I will try to tell you how it really was. Just not right now.

Be gentle on yourself

*****

 ## REFLECT:

How do you feel when you can't really articulate the busy-ness of your day, or the tiredness you feel?

What do you do to help unwind at the end of a busy day? How can you be gentle on yourself?

Who are you thankful to for asking how you are?

13th December

Over the years I've known several children who struggle with reading and writing, but who have an amazing flair for art. I got to see one of them today. Everything that seems to hold them back when working with words . . . that wading through treacle feeling, is totally absent, and they approach that new piece of paper with confidence and creativity as they explore different media. The lack of fluidity you can see when they read or write is replaced by a freedom of the hand; their stilted ideas are instead communicated with grace and eloquence, and you can literally see their self-belief rising as they draw or paint or create. I love seeing that freedom, that spark. It lights up their eyes. I love seeing the flicker grow into a flame that ignites something deeper in them, that encourages them and spurs them on to brighter things. I'm a firm believer in doing best what you love most. That thing that makes you tick, that gives you life, that you were somehow born to do, do that. If we can help children find their thing; if we can recognise it in them and help to call it out, to build it up, then I think that's a big part of our job done well.

Be someone who fans the flame

*****

REFLECT:

Think of a child who experiences difficulty in a particular area. What something else brings them to life?

How can you help children identify what they love? . . . and how can you encourage them to nurture it?

17th December

For a moment I saw the colour drain out of his face and his head just tilt down a little. You can literally see shame strip people of their poise. It was just a careless throw-away comment, not even unkind, and certainly not intended. It was just someone being in a hurry with something else on their minds and the non-recognition of something just hit this child like a truck. What the child had wanted in that moment was value, and appreciation, but busy-ness just got in the way and the moment slipped by.

Be watchful

*****

REFLECT:

Is there a moment when something similar has happened to you? . . . when you maybe hoped for a positive response from someone but somehow got something entirely different or no response at all? How did it leave you feeling?

How can we work to guard against these moments?

How can we support each other to be present in the moment?

18th December

Most days we help children to repair something that's broken. Today was no different. Restorative conversations and actions are so important when it comes to supporting children to regulate their emotions and navigate social interactions. It might be helping them find the words to repair something in a relationship with a peer; it might be helping them pick up the Lego bricks they threw angrily to the floor or making a start with helping them wipe off some graffiti they scribbled on the table. We come alongside them and give them the tools to help them fix what's broken or help bridge the divide. Without the assistance, the learning, some would find the damage unrepairable, the thought insurmountable, the gap too wide to cross; but doing it together to start with, somehow helps. Even as adults we're not always very good at saying 'I'm sorry', or 'I was wrong', but it's an essential life-skill for us all.

Be a restorer of broken things

*****

 REFLECT:

What do you find it hard to say sorry for? Why?

Who has helped come alongside you when you've felt a bit broken? What did that mean to you?

How do you come alongside children and families to help them restore broken things?

19th December

Today is a mixed day – it's the last day of term before the Christmas break. All the staff in school heave a sigh of relief, whilst also stocking up on prosecco or red wine (take your pick) and cough medicine in preparation for the juggernaut that hits your body once you finally stop and rest.

So, we've made it to the end of term – but it's also a sad day, for a loved-by-all colleague is leaving to venture pastures new. She's been with us for nearly two decades – and whilst in some places that might mean her practice is a bit stale, in her case, this is far from the truth. She feels a bit like the glue that holds the school together, and she carries a wealth of knowledge and experience. If the photocopier needs new toner, she's your first port of call. If you can't find any more paper clips, she's the person most likely to give you some of hers. She's one of the people who juggle their own workload as well as responding to the constant 'Can you just . . .'

But one of the most important things she does is her welcome. She's the first smiley face you see at the window as you approach the school office; if you're struggling to remember a name of a parent, she'll know who you mean; she knows people and remembers them, big facts and little facts alike . . . and people feel known. They feel like they belong. Although we're a large infant school, we aim for a 'small school feel', and everybody has a part to play. If you feel like an outsider, she's the kind of person you want to meet, because you feel drawn in; if you feel like you're different, instead you feel included. Though we tell her all the time, she's a builder of community without even realising.

Be a builder of community

*****

REFLECT:

What kind of greeting are your children and families met with? Is this consistent?

Who immediately puts people at ease in your school?

How do you create a sense of belonging and family in your school community?

Monthly musings

December – One of the crazy seasons

Parties, festivities, celebrations, rehearsals and performances . . . excited but tired children, busy and sometimes stressed parents, and colleagues who feel like they're on their knees. It's a busy time with lots of fun things going on, but everyone's also likely to be exhausted.

1 With different celebrations and festivities taking place usual routines are often disrupted at this time of year. Identify children who will find this difficult and discuss with them and their parents how best to prewarn them and help them cope with the changes they face. Seek to support them by integrating other kinds of structure or respite into their days.

2 Be aware of those who may experience this season with potential sensory overload and work with them and their parents to anticipate, eliminate or decrease potential stress points. Think of situations where you may have felt overwhelmed to try to empathise with some of their potential anxiety.

3 Relish the big and small successes. Recognise your hard work and investment in supporting children to join in with new and whole school seasonal events. When parents and carers laugh and cry and feel that enormous sense of pride at their children's achievements, you can take some of the credit and feel those emotions too.

4 Identify parents who may need reassurance around school performances or productions. Whilst some will eagerly look forward to seeing their child take part, others may be hesitant about how their child will cope, and others may find it difficult to have any differences sometimes publicly on show. Know your parents and have conversations about these things before the events. How can you make it work more easily for them and their child? Remember being inclusive is not about every child

doing or having the same, it's about meeting individual children's needs and supporting them to thrive within the school community.

5 If children are dressing up in costumes, be aware that this may increase some children's anxieties, whether that be through wearing unfamiliar clothes, with uncomfortable fits or heightened sensitivities around different fabrics, textures or labels and tags. Be creative, can the outfit be adapted? Does it have to be worn at all? Have discussions with children and parents about how best to manage these potential stress points.

6 With changes to routines, the logistics of using different spaces in schools for different activities needs additional planning and communication. Communicate changes well to alleviate potential clashes and keep things running smoothly. If staff are tired, any unintended miscommunications can cause added tension at this point in the term.

7 Recognise how shattered you all are. Give each other grace and recognise that you're all doing above and beyond at this time.

8 How can you encourage each other right now when everything feels so busy?

9 Pace yourself as you head towards the end of term. Build in moments of rest amongst the busy.

10 Celebrate well when you get to the end. . . . You deserve it!

NOTES – My musings . . .

 January

4th January

Why is it that people have to shout really loud to get themselves heard? Why is it that the people who know an individual the best; who cater for their child's needs 24/7; who know what it's like to cope with their child's emotional distress when plans are suddenly cancelled beyond their control; who know what it is to spend hours settling their child to sleep every . . . single . . . night because their child's anxiety is through the roof, and then they have to start all over again in the morning. . . . Why is it that they often have to keep on asking, keep on badgering, day in day out to make their plea, to get seen for an appointment, to stay on a waiting list, to express their concern? Why is it that they often don't feel heard at all and feel that they have to fight? Fight before funding is granted, before resources are released, before some kind of respite comes.

I was sat this morning with a mum who feels like she's not got much fight left. I'm pretty sure she'll have some tomorrow, but right now she's running on empty. She just wants her voice to be heard. She just wants the best for her child, and we're working together to make this happen, but it's so very hard for her today. We're here to listen and offer support, but sometimes, when things are beyond our control, that just looks like really good listening. So, she can say what she thinks, say how she feels and know that she's been heard.

Be attentive

*****

DOI: 10.4324/9781003333753-6

REFLECT:

How do you feel when you have to fight for something?
Who are you working with at the moment that's in this kind of place?
How can you as a school create time, space and support for them?

7th January

Staffroom talk today was about how many of us wake in the middle of the night and then find it difficult to get back to sleep, because the 'to do' list takes over. We joked about the notepads we have at the side of the bed to jot down our ideas, in the hope that it will free up our brains to then get back to sleep. Teachers and support staff work really hard. I mean *really* hard. We have to encourage each other. Encourage people for all the time and effort they put in to meeting the needs of the children in their care, for all the mini adjustments they make all of the time, for all their sleepless nights, all their coming up with alternative ideas to try to make things better for children, for all the resources they pick up when they see something that might help when they're out and about, for all their grappling with differentiating the curriculum so that it meets the needs of their children. We need to get better at saying well done. It's not that we don't want to say it. It's that we're all just so busy. We've got to be intentional about it and create time to have these conversations.

I remember a long time ago in a previous school, an Educational Psychologist congratulating me for the turnaround of a ten-year old's behaviour. David had been at risk of exclusion for a number of terms, and then since midway through the Autumn term of Year Six, had suddenly seemed so much more settled. I knew the change wasn't really my doing at all. It was all to do with the change in his class teacher. He had gone from having a more 'old school' kind of teacher to a young NQT (Newly Qualified Teacher), new and fresh to the job. The former teacher had had little flexibility about her practice – although countless discussions had been had with her about adapting some of her strategies and language, but she just wasn't on board. She'd been teaching for years, and I was a young upstart of a SENCO at the time who was challenging her way of doing things and suggesting alternative ways of working. The trouble was, so many of her interactions with the child just fuelled tricky behaviour.

Contrast to his new teacher – who was more willing to look at what was going on behind it all; who used positive phrasing; gave limited choices, maintained clear and consistent responses; had high expectations; gave a sense of responsibility and worked hard to develop the child's self-esteem, and as a result, trust began to grow. When children's behaviour is tricky, we first have to examine what we're all doing, and be prepared to change our responses where it's needed. I relished passing on to the new teacher what had been said about the change in the child. Praise where praise is due.

Be an encourager

*****

REFLECT:

How can you encourage another member of staff today?
What would you like someone to notice about what you've done today?

8th January

I woke up today with a rotten cold. Nose blocked, sinuses bursting and senses dulled. I feel like I can't hear properly. Disorientated. Words are muffled, sentences unclear and I just want to hide myself away. I'm having to work hard to read facial expressions. I keep asking people to repeat what they've said. I'm suddenly aware of how much I'm relying on reading people's lips or looking at their lip patterns. Ordinarily, I don't even think about these things. I take communication for granted. But today it's made me think again about people with hearing impairment and some of the barriers they face on a daily basis. I've had the privilege of working in a mainstream school with enhanced provision for children and families with hearing impairment. But I wonder if sometimes we can get so used to the practice and provision around us that we forget to try and put ourselves in other people's shoes. It'll never be the same experience, but it helps to try.

Be someone who tries to put yourself in someone else's shoes

*****

REFLECT:

Whose shoes could you try on?

What might it teach you about their life experience and how it differs from yours?

9th January

It's census return time, where we summarise information and data about what the SEND picture looks like in our school. How many children have different kinds of level of support, and what the different categories of need look like. That kind of thing. And every time it causes me to think, because I have to fit a child into a box. I have to state a primary area of need. I have to prioritise one need over another.

Language is important. It empowers. It creates opportunity. It challenges prejudice and discrimination. And so, I sometimes struggle with the whole language around SEND . . . Take the word DISability. It's a DIS attached to being able. I've known many children who are classed as DIS but are very able, in all sorts of ways. Whenever you attach a DIS to something it has the danger of communicating something less than. Dis-interested, dis-associated, dis-connected. . . . It's a bit like the prefix UN . . . if you're not careful the connotation lends itself to something negative. Un-comfortable, un-helpful, un-mentionable. . .

On the other hand, there's the language of neurodiversity. Having something to do with 'diversity' conjures up images of life and light, colour and sound, of complex patterns and systems, of equality, of variety and difference which has creative breath running right through it. It has the feel of a mind-boggling physicist explaining how galaxies work, or a biologist gushing over the intricacies of the living world. Diversity in all its beauty.

In schools we all have to be united. We have to make sure we speak the same language, otherwise things can get lost in translation. Things can get missed. Things can get misunderstood, misrepresented or mistaken.

Be united

*****

 REFLECT:

How consistent is the language you all use in your school community?

Think about the language you use when you describe children's needs and strengths. Do they tell the whole story?

Are they words you would like to hear if they were being said about you?

10th January

I called a Mum today to say how well her child had coped with his morning. The silent relief in her voice was deafening. Parents of children who often experience unsettled behaviour get so used to hearing about the times when things are not going so well. They hear it from school. They hear it in the playground. They hear it from other parents and other children. They hear it from the lack of invites to other children's parties. They hear it from well-meaning or 'embarrassed' family members. They hear it in the raised eyebrows of people they don't even know in the shopping aisle. As a parent or carer, if you see your child's school phone number come up as you take the call, our 'go to' response is that something's wrong. Otherwise, why would they be calling? It doesn't have to be like this. Taking the time to call people when things are going well can mean so much.

Be a bearer of good news

*****

 REFLECT:

Think about when you've been in a conversation where you felt awkwardness or shame or guilt or hopelessness. What could have made that conversation feel different?

Who could you encourage this week with a call about something going well?

14th January

Teachers and LSAs (Learning Support Assistants) are like octopuses. Or is that octopi? Moving around the class, a nod and a wink here, a discrete thumbs up there, a tap on the paper to refocus a child here, a smile to praise, picking up on a child's misconceptions here, clarifying an instruction there, modelling a new strategy, prompting recall of something learnt before, assisting with developing self-help skills – eating, dressing, toileting; boosting self-esteem, alleviating anxiety, stepping in to de-escalate tricky behaviour, delivering interventions, unpicking observations, assessing learning to inform planning . . . arms and eyes everywhere . . . and that's just while the children are actually in the room. No wonder everyone's exhausted at the end of the day. I think it's sometimes helpful to recognise the enormity of what we do every single day, and just be kind to ourselves.

Be kind to yourself

*****

 REFLECT:

How can you be kind to yourself today?

How could you show the same to a colleague?

15th January

That felt uncomfortable. I want to do my job well, but today I've been found wanting. Not even really by someone else, but mainly by me. Just a little thing that's easily rectified, a phone call that needs to be made sooner rather than later, but there's still a sense of regret, a sense of 'I wish I'd handled that better'. I know I'm feeling tired so the whole thing probably feels bigger than it is, but right now I feel the offence, I feel the discomfort.

Sometimes being a SENCO feels like undergoing surgery. You feel exposed . . . vulnerable . . . on the operating table waiting to go under. It can happen when a long-awaited appointment that has been looming on the horizon suddenly arrives, (just think some kind of inspection); or in some unsuspecting moment that pops up on any given day. It's an occasion when you find your work, and more painfully yourself, being scrutinised. Like someone is leaning over you in full PPE (personal protective equipment), scalpel in hand, about to dissect your every word, action, examining it all on the table, looking for where things are healthy but also where things are not. Looking for areas of dysfunction and areas of potential disease. It doesn't feel nice going under the knife. It's easy to take things personally when questions are asked that make us feel uncomfortable, when we fumble our words, when explanations we give are deemed to be lacking. Professional conversations can be dreaded. We know they're intended to refine our practice and help us see our blind spots. The problem comes on occasions when scrutiny comes with blame rather than support. When scrutiny brings shame rather than hope. They're not helpful conversations at all.

Over the years I've been trying to learn to approach these moments with less fear. Perhaps fear is too strong a word, although sometimes the thought of them has kept me awake at night. Butterflies in the stomach might be more apt, although let's not belittle it to the children's game 'Operation' with plastic butterflies in cavities that need to be taken out with tweezers. We are real living people, so scrutiny and surgery can feel a lot weightier than that. But if we know our children well, know their progress and challenges, if we regularly examine our systems and their effectiveness, we can come to these discussions with a sense of peace, prepared to offer

explanations that are not excuses, and to give information that provides context and understanding.

Be reflective

*****

 REFLECT:

How do you approach professional conversations where your work is observed or under scrutiny?

How do they make you feel as you anticipate them, engage with them and then reflect afterwards?

How do you feel when you identify areas that you need to develop as well as areas you regard as strengths?

16th January

Sometimes a day starts normally, but within seconds becomes something entirely different. A day that starts as ordinary or even mundane suddenly becomes one filled with a sense of ominous threat, and a normal day of the week becomes one that is more about life and death, etched in our memory for all the wrong reasons. Personally, I don't tend to think about death very much, not on a day-to-day basis, but that might not be the case for some of our families who have children in school with medical conditions. On any given 'normal' day their conditions can mean they are at higher risk of illness. For some, managing their conditions literally is a matter of life and death.

This morning I had a meeting with some parents about their child's newly diagnosed medical condition. Maybe it had been lying there hidden under the surface all along, but now it's just appeared, somehow activated out of the blue. It's been a surprise for the whole family, and now that surprise falls with us. In these situations, we discuss things comprehensively with parents and the children themselves and have care plans and risk assessments in place for those who need them; protective measures that will keep them safe. We always talk about how parents have to feel confident that we will meet their children's needs and so feel able to entrust them to our care. It's a big responsibility for the whole staff team, and one we take very seriously, working with the expertise of health professionals to learn the skills we need, to ensure that everyone is safe. Whenever I have these discussions, I'm always struck by the reality that for some of our school community the potential of facing serious health difficulties or even loss of life, is something they have to live with every day. For many of us, we so often have this kind of assumption in life that we're somehow immortal, until something comes along that brings a different perspective. Right now, I'm hyper aware that we need to protect this child. There's no room for error. It feels daunting, and rightly so, but we will work together to give this child what they need.

Be protective

*****

REFLECT:

Think about children you know who have medical conditions that require additional support. Think about the emotional needs that may accompany their diagnosis. How do you as a school community reassure them that they are safe?

How do you build trust with parents and carers, so that they can entrust their children into your care?

How do you build staff confidence and expertise in supporting children with medical conditions?

17th January

Lights, camera, action! At lunchtime, rehearsals are in full flow for a parent meeting later this evening. When I say rehearsals, I mean a speedy re-reading of bullet points and presentation notes whilst eating your lunch. Tonight, it's a meeting with a hall full of prospective parents and some members of staff feel more confident at speaking in this kind of context than others. The truth is, we have skilled experienced teachers who have no problem at all standing up in front of their classes or a hall full of children every day but having to get up and deliver a spiel to parents or to other professionals outside of the context of your own school can often feel more awkward, or for some even nerve-wracking. None of us really come into this job for the fame, or for the spotlight to be on us. So that feeling of all eyes on you can feel a bit uncomfortable.

I'm wondering though if it's a glimpse into what some children experience when they feel put on the spot. Even with something as 'everyday' and apparently non-threatening as that age-old speaking and listening practice of Show and Tell, where children are invited to show something special to their peers or talk about an experience or something important to them. Some children relish the attention and are first to volunteer to speak; some have a special something they want to tell everyone about; others find something random they've come across moments before and make it up on the spot, but for others it can be a moment they dread. A please don't pick me moment. Much like tonight. An all eyes on me moment. It's the butterflies in the stomach. The dry mouth and losing your way with your words.

Sometimes we do things outside of our comfort zones and in the process discover something new or see something from a different perspective. It's something we always need to press into, but we also need to note the discomfort.

Be a seer of different perspectives

*****

REFLECT:

What do you sometimes have to press into that you don't like?
When you've got through it how do you feel? What did you learn?
What different perspective did you grasp?

18th January

Sometimes in this job you feel like you're target practice. Like you've got a big red bullseye painted on you and you're just waiting for the next arrow to whizz its way through the air and land with a 'Thwang!' Some days it feels like they launch at you one after another, causing you to wince and brace yourself for the next incoming. Most of the time they don't hit the bullseye, and maybe just score a peripheral 4 or 5 so don't sting that much. But sometimes, one hits you dead centre and you feel struck. Sometimes they come from parents, sometimes from other professionals or colleagues.

Before I'd even really had a chance to fire up my laptop this morning, I'd already taken a couple of hits, and it felt like it was going to be one of those days. People don't necessarily mean to take aim, but by very nature of the job we do, sometimes we and the people around us are under stress. I often don't hear about things when everything's ticking along nicely . . . but I sure do hear about things when things are going wrong, or just a bit awry. The 'offence' might only be something little in the grand scheme of things . . . some minor mishap maybe, but by the time there have been a few of those, it can all start to feel a bit bigger if you're feeling a bit fragile. Any kind of middle or senior leadership role comes with the risk. It's in the job description. People say you have to develop a thick skin, or words to that effect. I understand where they're coming from but I'm not sure that always helps. I get it that you need to feel protected so that you don't get taken down, but if arrows just bounce off you and it looks like you're not interested in the offence or don't really care, it doesn't help relationships going forwards. I have found you have to listen well, help bring other perspectives and give context, work together to find solutions and also be ready to say sorry when needed. That's me with my big girl pants on. Right now, I'm going home to grab a cup of tea and nurse my wounds.

Become skilled at conflict resolution

*****

 REFLECT:

How do you feel when you are in a 'conflict' conversation? How do you prepare?

How do you respond in the moment? Do you tend to be defensive, want to go on the offense or do you take a different posture?

How can you practise being open to what is being said, and open in how you respond?

21st January

6.30am – The weather warnings were right, and we've got snow. I love snow! I love the anticipation of it. I love the eery sky when it's about to fall. I love watching the big thick flakes and noticing the quiet as it blankets the roads and muffles the noise of the traffic. I love wrapping up warm and heading out into it making fresh footprints and feeling the cold on my face.

I love all these things about snow, but it's not so pretty when it goes slushy and dirty at the side of the roads or when it freezes to ice overnight, and if I have the choice, I don't like driving in it. Our school pretty much always stays open. We rarely have snow days where it shuts, so this morning I get up that bit earlier to give myself time to do the normally forty-minute walk to work instead. I factor in a bit more time because I might be a bit unsteady underfoot, and off I set, like an Arctic explorer.

The thing about snow that I sometimes forget is the disruption it causes. Usual routines suddenly feel more complex, and more planning is needed, and I know that for some of our families just getting to school at the normal start-time each day is challenging enough. So, factor in a bit of snow and we might have some families arriving a bit more stressed than usual. What I know is that for some of our families just getting out of the house can feel like a mission in itself, even on a 'normal' day. And yes, there's that question again . . . what even *is* normal? Some will already have had stress around what's on the dinner menu today; some won't be able to take for granted that their child will hold onto the buggy and not run off into the road if they see something that interests them; some will have to navigate turn-taking about who sits where in the car; some will be exhausted from trying to help their child get dressed and remember what they need. And today, some will also have children who don't like this strange thing that's falling from the sky or the fact that everything's turned white; some will have children who just don't like the cold or wearing hats or gloves because they're not used to them or the label is too itchy; some will have children who have mobility difficulties at the best of times let alone on slippery surfaces.

I can easily take my normal routine, my normal experience, for granted. So even though I'll arrive with time to spare and be able to warm up and grab a quick cup of tea before the start of the school day, some of our families will arrive feeling like they've done a real expedition. So, we'll all be in teams on the door to welcome them, congratulate them, reassure them and help them thaw out.

Be someone who doesn't take things for granted

*****

 ## REFLECT:

What do you think you sometimes take for granted?

How do some of your children's needs impact on them and their families on a daily basis?

22nd January

This morning was hard. Necessary but hard.

It can feel hard to have tough conversations. Even if we have to steel ourselves for them because it's just part of our job, we need to treat them with care. Sometimes we speak with parents, and we know that just by talking about what's working but then venturing on to 'what might not be working so well' . . . just by having the 'but', we're venturing into scary territory. For some perhaps there's been a niggling thought playing at the back of their mind, where they've noticed their child does things or doesn't do things like other children, whether that be siblings or friends' children or just watching other children out and about. For some parents, they may have pushed their thoughts down beneath the surface because they seem too worrying to entertain; for others, any mention of possible additional things to consider may come as a bolt out of the blue; and for others it's sometimes a welcome relief that someone else has noticed something too, and the parent feels that they're not going mad or second guessing themselves or making things up. The difficulty is, especially in those early conversations, we may not know how the parent may feel about it all until we knock on the door, so to speak. So, we have to knock gently rather than come barging in. For many parents just having these kinds of conversations can make them feel vulnerable and laid bare.

When we talk about how children are doing, if there's a leaning towards a 'but', then we know it might well be hard for someone to hear. If we express concerns, just the word 'concerns' can convey something negative; something potentially 'less than'. It can so easily feed into a deficit mindset. Perhaps we need to try to find a new word. A new language. We live in a culture of comparison. It's not helpful or healthy, and sometimes it's even dangerous. It's never about this child versus another. We need to focus on the one in front of us, with all their strengths as well as the things they find difficult, and for some parents we need to help them do the same.

It's about wanting the best for their child and having the conversation carefully.

Be someone who carefully presses into sensitive conversations

*****

 REFLECT:

How do you prepare for conversations like these?

What kind of language do you use when you're talking about strengths and needs, or what's working and not working so well?

Monthly musings

January – Braving the winter

Cold long dark days. January can feel like a long slog of a month, with the holiday period now behind everyone. Families and colleagues will have had varying experiences during this time and the season may well have been hectic. Children, parents and colleagues may be returning to school with a variety of emotions as we all regather ourselves and engage again in school routines.

1 The new year can be an intentional time to detox and refocus with a new resolve. Think back to that initial idea of who you want to be and what you want to bring to your team and those you work with. How is that going?

2 Reflect on your own experience over the holiday break. What feelings are you left with? If the season was busy, how rested are you as you face another term?

3 In relationships or interactions where things feel stuck, consider what might help them get unstuck. Is there something you could do to get things moving or shift the dynamic?

4 Make space for conversations with parents who may have found the holiday period difficult. Explore possible feelings of disappointment at this time, where the holiday period perhaps fell short of their hopes and instead, they were faced with a different reality, where they may have had to cope with the harsh voice of comparison or increased tiredness due to supporting their children through changes in routine.

They may have felt an added pressure of 'managing' their child's behaviour within wider family gatherings, with all the potential tuts and sighs or raised eyebrows that can come with a different perception or lack of understanding around children's needs, different expectations and different thinking about how to parent. In wider family situations with special occasions and different family traditions, interactions can feel more intense. Pressing into these conversations with parents continues to build trust and shows your understanding of their and their children's needs.

5 Review your action plans and progress towards outcomes. Recast vision for any next steps ahead and celebrate your achievements so far.

6 The Spring term is the shortest of the year, and before you know it you'll be heading towards the Easter holidays, so plan your priorities for the next few weeks.

7 With the fun of December over and waiting for Spring, think about parents who are in that ongoing relentless process of waiting, maybe for appointments or assessments, decisions or diagnoses, support or funding. How can you touch base with them or encourage them at this time?

8 What do you need to pick up again or chase or push for after the holiday in order to advocate for the children and families you work with?

9 This term can be one where for some children things just seem to 'click' and you see them making new connections and leaps of progress in their learning and skills. Remember to look back at their starting points and recognise how far they've come. Remind parents and children to do the same.

10 Another census return time. Look again at the cohort of children you currently have. Think about the language you and your colleagues use when identifying children's needs. When you categorise areas of need, examine how this then leads to provision that meets individual needs. Consider the anxiety that some parents have, that if a need is identified this might potentially, even if unintentionally, box children in.

NOTES – My musings . . .

📅 February

4th February

'I can read! I can read!' The belief that little Harvey suddenly expressed today felt like his success had happened overnight. Truth is, it was happening because of his hard work and the hard work, support and careful planning of those around him over many days and weeks . . . but the celebration was totally his . . . his resilience, his making a start at each reading activity every day, his daily moments of challenge, his effort and persistence even when it was so very hard, even when nothing seemed to click. And look at him now! He looked a foot taller. It's amazing what self-belief does, what confidence looks like. You can literally see it.

We talk with children about what they *can* do a lot, and about what might be tricky for them at the moment . . . that they might not be able to do something *yet*, but as they keep practising and keep going, the neurons in their brains start firing and making new connections and pathways that over time birth new skills and understanding. We know that confidence is such an important foundation to learning, but every day we partake in this delicate balancing act. Because when it comes to children with additional needs, all the while we're celebrating what they can now do, what they've achieved and what progress they've made, the system also still requires us to evidence areas of need, areas of perceived lack, especially when it comes to seeking funding or diagnoses. It's not supposed to, but it can still feel like the whole system functions on a logarithm of deficit.

So I now have the job of writing up this child's Annual Review paperwork, and whilst he has shown increasing independence, confidence and progress, (and of course that's what we all want; that's what we're in the job for), people who know him well also know that there is a risk his level of funding might decrease or even be stopped altogether if I don't choose my words carefully as I write. And that would be ok if we felt his progress would still

DOI: 10.4324/9781003333753-7

continue, but it just feels a bit too early to know that for sure; that his resilience is not quite steady enough to be sustained without some kind of support. Sometimes you almost feel like you have to water down a child's successes so that progress is still noted, but so is their need . . . and that never sits quite right with me. Sometimes the system just feels a bit broken, and although I can voice it in SENCO forums and with Local Authority representatives, it feels like my place is just a bit too little in the grand scheme of things to see anything change. So, with little Harvey in mind, I'm going to try my best to get the balance as I write.

Be balanced

*****

 REFLECT:

Think about your own strengths and areas of development. What would you like others to say about you?

How do you navigate the balance of describing strengths and needs when you're painting the picture of a child?

What parts of the wider system do you sometimes feel are like a misfit, or grate against inclusion rather than help facilitate it?

5th February

Sometimes I feel like the multi-faceted master of disguise! So many parts to play. So many costume changes. . . . A detective looking for clues with magnifying glass in hand; a surgeon dissecting different aspects of what might be going on for a child, analysing each layer under a microscope; a counsellor, helping people to make connections and providing them with safe spaces to explore their thinking; a logistics supervisor, organising what resources are available and when; a recruitment agency involved in securing qualified or keen-to-learn staff; a care worker supporting with toileting and self-care needs; a data analyst, a fundraiser, to name but a few and oh gosh, I nearly forgot – a teacher!

Today has been crazy. So many different things to do, and I'm not sure I've done any of it very well. I feel I might have got some of my costume changes a bit muddled because there was just not enough time in between. It's been a day of speed-walking down the corridor (because we walk in school and don't run) to get to my next meeting, or to answer the phone, or to catch a member of staff, or to encourage a child or speak with a parent. Whizzing what feels like all day from one thing to the next, with no space to catch my breath in between. So, at the end of the day, here I am, just flopped in the chair, unable to move. Props and costumes strewn all over the floor ready to be hung up and put away for another day. They'll just have to wait a bit while I recover . . . regroup . . . and get rehearsing my lines for tomorrow.

Be multi-faceted

*****

REFLECT:

Think about all the costume changes you do within any given day. Think about all the skills you use and all the different functions you perform.

When you feel like your day has been a bit of a blur, try to identify one thing of which to be proud.

6th February

Year One have their school trip coming up next month to a local outdoor activity centre, and we're all in the throes of planning. Pre-visits to the site, conversations with specific children, parents teachers and LSA's about risk assessments, provision, access and all the other preparation involved. I love it that staff know the children so well and automatically think about the different or additional things that need to be included in the discussions. Access to a peanut ball, or another piece of specific equipment; access to a breakout, calming space where sensory needs can be met; access to whole class or individual visual timetables; access to photos of the new environment and activities that will happen to prepare children for the differences in the day ahead. Making learning opportunities and experiences accessible for all involves remembering the individuals in the planning, and everyone mucking in to make it happen.

Be a creator of access

*****

REFLECT:

Think of a time when you've not been able to access something you wanted to. How has that left you feeling?

How do you make activities and experiences accessible to all in your setting?

Are there further ways you could improve your provision and accessibility?

7th February

This morning one of our classes had a special assembly. It was an impromptu one, organised to give a child an opportunity to share his talent. This quiet, unassuming little boy, usually awkward in the company of others, whose Mum would often describe as being in his own little world, sat down at the piano and played this masterpiece. No music to follow, just all in his head and his fingers, and there were gasps of awe around the room. You could literally hear a pin drop when he stopped as people took in what had just happened . . . and then there was applause . . . and then he beamed.

If we're not careful, some children don't get a chance to shine in school. Not because they're somehow dull or incapable of shining, but because education often focuses on things they find more tricky or less interesting. Schools need to be places that nurture creativity. Regardless of the relentless pressure for children to progress and achieve in core subjects we must still fight to be hubs of creativity where music and the arts and sport have space to breathe. Shining for one child might look completely different to another. We need to find and create moments where all children have a chance to shine. They're moments worth singing about.

Be a facilitator of shine!

*****

 REFLECT:

Think of a child who finds some aspects of learning difficult. How can you create space for them to shine this week?

How can you weave more consistent opportunities or moments for creativity into your class this week?

Where do you shine?

8th February

I watched a video today that a teacher had recorded to show Max's mum. It was a slow-motion clip of him running into a pyramid of stacking cups he'd taken ages to build. The pyramid was taller than him. The joy was that he wasn't running into it in any kind of fit of rage; instead, he was like a victor with outstretched arms running through the finishing tape at the end of a race, proud of his achievements. Just building the stacking cups had been momentous for him. He finds it so difficult to face any element of challenge for fear of it not living up to what he wants. He has an idea of what he wants something to look like, and if he considers it to fall short in any way, this can trigger big outbursts of distress and anger. His teacher has been working on the stacking cups thing with him for a while now; encouraging him to build them together with her; one by one; taking it in turns; working together to adjust them when one looks a bit wobbly; picking them up and stacking them up again when one tumbles. There'd been times when he'd give up early on, or couldn't face the challenge at all, but each small step of practice each tackling it together with her by his side has led to today's success. Tomorrow might be different again, but today we glimpsed some resilience. Yes!!

Be a builder of resilience

*****

REFLECT:

Consider some children in your school. What recent moments of resilience can you celebrate?

Think of something you've really persevered at over the years. Think about the feelings you felt along the way . . . when it first seemed impossible, when the skill felt too hard, when it took so long to feel like you were getting anywhere, to a sense of achievement. . . . Think of a child who might be on a similar journey at the moment. What feelings might they be experiencing?

How do you communicate children's effort and successes to your parents and carers? Are there more ways you could bring some of these to life to somehow capture the moment more fully?

11th February

There was a point today where I came off the phone feeling so angry. I mean *really* angry. Like so angry it took up all my thinking and feeling and I couldn't move on from it for a while.

Trying to access additional funding for individual children can be so hard. You have to submit evidence so that they, the people who hold the purse strings, will believe you. Believe your case. Believe that you're not making it up. I know that's not really what they're doing, but sometimes it can certainly feel like it. Sometimes it feels like a 'them' and 'us' scenario. Prosecutor and defendant. It shouldn't, but it does.

Why would any of us in our job try to apply for funding if we didn't really think we needed it for a child?! Why would we be asking for more money to release resources if we hadn't tried everything we could think of before? I know that budgets everywhere are stretched, but today it just felt like where's the trust? Where's the recognition of our professional judgement? I talked to my Head-teacher about it, and she was as cross as I was.

I've been thinking, and it might be a bit simplistic, but I kind of think that maybe the whole system could work a bit better if people who make 'high up' decisions about education and SEND (Special Educational Needs and Disability) actually have some kind of experience in education or with SEND themselves? Have they ever actually stood in a class and taught?! If there were people who really knew (not just pretend knowing, or from-a-distance knowing) what it's like to be in a classroom trying to meet the needs of 30 children, some of whom have additional and highly complex needs – people who really understood that it's not just these individual needs but also the complex interplay they present in the dynamic of the classroom – that different children with different needs are like the number of different combinations you can get on a lock, where on any given day and in any given moment the combination can change again. It's not as simple as looking at one individual child's needs at a time. Sometimes the collective whole needs to be considered when funding is being discussed.

Be able to let off steam!

*****

REFLECT:

What challenges do you face around funding?

What does it feel like when you don't feel believed or trusted . . . and how does that impact on the way you work with the parties involved?

Do you have trusted people that you can go to in confidence to let off steam?

12th February

A few weeks ago, I opened an email giving me information about a child with an EHCP (Education Health and Care Plan) who had just moved into the area and wanted to come to our school. The paperwork was not a quick read. There were lengthy, multisyllabic, medical references and technical terms about his health conditions that meant we have had a lot to digest to ensure we put in the right provision he needs. The consultation paperwork needed returning promptly, so my mind started whirring from the off. This child has required bespoke, detailed transition planning around his needs, with input from him, his parents and multiple other professionals.

So, that was the paperwork . . . but then this morning I got to meet the boy! In the flesh, in person, with his mum . . . and oh how the paperwork didn't do him justice! When you read what's written about a child, you build up a picture of them in your mind. That's what's supposed to happen, so that you can make all the preparations that are needed. But what we need to remember is the picture is always 2D. It's always just print on paper. Or words from a discussion. It's never in full technicolour, with surround sound. However well written the paperwork is, there will always be an element of lack . . . because when you finally get to meet the living, breathing person themselves, it's a totally different experience. It's the difference between reading a script and seeing the play.

This young man was an absolute delight. He had this spark about him that I just know will endear him to many. His sense of humour and love of life is tangible . . . and what struck me was the complete inability of the words on the paper to prepare you for meeting him in all his glory. However hard they tried it was never going to be able to fully capture the entirety, the essence of him. However person-centred and well-written EHCP documents are (and sadly, some are left wanting), we need to create space to let the words we read come to life, and to allow ourselves to be surprised, so that any picture we have created in our minds eye can be blown out of the water when we meet someone in person.

We want that for ourselves, right?! If someone introduces you to someone else and you're met with an 'Oh, so and so's told me so much about you!', you always wonder what they've actually been told. I mean, what little bit of me has been communicated? And would I say the same?! Does it really capture who I am?

Be ready to be surprised

*****

REFLECT:

What are the most important things you want others to know about you?

Have you ever met someone and come away with a totally different impression of them to the one you had before you met? What did that experience tell you about yourself or them?

How can you create and hold a picture of someone in your mind's eye, whilst giving it space to breathe and be something other or bigger than the space it currently holds?

14th February

Today we said goodbye to an LSA (Learning Support Assistant) who's been with us for years. There was shared excitement about her new job opportunities ahead, but also sadness at her leaving, and amongst it all, fond, fond memories of shared times. Good times. Throughout the years there has been ongoing discussion and close scrutiny of the effectiveness of LSA support, with teachers being monitored carefully around their deployment of additional adults in the room, and everyone having to evidence the impact of their provision on outcomes for children. LSA support is always about developing children's independence, and staff have to be skilled to ensure that any support they give does not lead to reliance on them. It's about providing a resource to resource the child.

This morning I had the privilege of observing a child giving fleeting joint attention to an activity with an adult for a few seconds. It was a moment of shared participation. It was one of those moments where I love my job . . . and the LSA was blown away too. So much hard work had gone into getting to that point. So much planning and rehearsal. We, like so many schools, are fortunate to have a team of highly skilled support staff, as well as some that are new to the job, but rapidly gaining experience. It was the skill of the practitioner over time, that had led to that moment of achievement. Not just in our school, but historically, support staff roles have often been pursued by parents of children in school, because obviously it's convenient if your work hours roughly match with your children's and having a term-time job has childcare advantages . . . but the role of a teaching assistant is unrecognisable from years ago. Where in the long and distant past a support assistant might have helped with things such as hearing children read or doing sewing or cooking; putting up displays, washing up paint pots and gathering resources; they are now so much more. LSA's are trained practitioners, in the thick of supporting pupil wellbeing and learning, and often supporting some of our most vulnerable children, with a multitude of additional needs. They have to be skilled at scaffolding tasks and communicating, at observing and recording, at moving learning on, diffusing conflict and so, so much more. They are skilled members of the team, and yet can often feel undervalued. The truth is they are paid pitifully for what they do. Their pay doesn't reflect their expertise or their efforts, but it's how the general pay structure and system is currently set up. So, where there's a gap around pay and recognition, let's be people who plug that gap, who encourage and speak out the skills of those around us. Let's 'notice' the things that can go unnoticed. Let's notice the people who may sometimes feel unnoticed. Let's express value and let's spur each other on.

Be someone who values others

*****

REFLECT:

How do you feel when you feel unseen?

How do you feel when your efforts and skills are noticed by others . . . and what impact does it have on you and your work?

How do you express value to others? Are there ways you can be more intentional about communicating this?

15th February

'I feel so angry it's like my head's going to explode like a volcano!' he said. Breakthrough! Words that convey how he's feeling rather than him just displaying his anger via a physical response. This is a little one who can find it difficult to regulate his emotions, but he's come such a long way. Instead of real-life fiery lava spewing out, this time it was words.

There are hundreds of words to describe our feelings and emotions, and the more we know, the more emotionally literate we become. So today I was exploring emotions vocabulary with this child. We went over some basics and then started to think about degrees of emotion, as if they're on a sliding scale. There are plenty of toolkits and programmes out there to help develop emotional regulation skills, but the key is that the child begins to recognise emotions in themselves and others 'in the moment', in real-life, in the here and now . . . and words really help. Once they can begin to pinpoint their feelings and the physiological responses in their own bodies, they can begin to anticipate them, understand what helps them and identify what tools they can use to regulate them.

As adults, we can feel a whole range of emotions within our school days, so we need to be just as aware of what's going on for us and how our feelings might also be impacting on others. We have days full of highs and lows and everything in between when you work in a school. On any given day with the varied nature of the role, I can feel any of the following:

A-amazed/anxious, B – brave/bored, C – courageous/concerned, D – delighted/dissatisfied, E – excited/exasperated, F – fascinated/ frustrated, G – grateful/guilty, H – hopeful/hesitant, I – interested/irritated, J – joyful/jaded, K – kind-hearted/ (a bit of a) killjoy, L – liked/lonely, M – magical/mad, N – nurturing/nervous, O – optimistic/overwhelmed, P – passionate/panic-ed, Q – quiet/ quarrelsome, R – relieved/resigned, S – surprised/shocked, T – triumphant/timid, U – ultra-happy/uncomfortable, V – vigilant/ vulnerable, W – (in) wonder/weary, X – 'extra' any of the above, Y – yearning/yappy, Z – (full of) zest/zealous. . . .

Be emotionally literate

*****

REFLECT:

When was the last time you were so angry you thought you might erupt? Consider how this same intensity of emotion may be felt by children and adults with whom we work.

What emotions have you felt today/this week?

How can you make space for emotions to be expressed in a safe way?

25th February

Today I was having a bit of a clear out whilst eating my lunch. I've got this collection of random things in my office on my shelf. Anyone walking in might think it very eclectic. At the moment, some of the collection consists of a metal hedgehog from a garden centre that wobbles on a stand; a ceramic pot that looks like it's made out of pencils that's been glued together, but still comes apart down the middle if it's knocked; a glittery plaque; a picture that's been hastily drawn. They're things that I treasure and won't be throwing out any time soon. Each one's been given to me by a child at the end of term . . . and each one tells a story . . . and I think the stories are really important. They're important to remember, and important to draw on. Each one tells of a journey; of a plot that unfolded with twists and turns; of a focal character that you've travelled with. As a teacher, LSA or SENCO you get to be a collector of stories, and over the years you end up with a huge compendium of treasured tales. At some point the knick-knacks that remind you of the people behind the stories might rust, or decay, but the stories live on!

Be a collector of stories

*****

 ## REFLECT:

What stories have you collected? Think of children you currently work with or have worked with over the years. Think about why specific children come to mind.

What do you recall first and foremost about them? What did you invest in them? What did you learn?

How do these stories impact on how you feel about your job and what you do?

26th February

Today was a case of eating humble pie with a colleague. I'd said I was going to do something yesterday, and I just didn't get round to it. It wasn't intentional, and certainly wasn't deliberate. I'd just found myself squeezed for time and hadn't been able to do what I'd said I would. Maybe next time I need to consider if I really do have time to do that something before I say I will. Or maybe I need to give the caveat that I will *try* to do it, because in this role something often just 'comes up' that means I have to roll over some (or sometimes most) of my to-do-list to another day. Regardless of the circumstances, my colleague was a bit miffed because my inaction had just made something a bit more complicated for her. Sometimes I have a bit of an internal dialogue going on, like 'you have no idea how crazy my day was yesterday', 'you literally have no clue what I was up against, what came out of the blue, what I had to prioritise' . . . and although all these things may be true, sometimes you know in that moment, that it doesn't help to voice them. What *might* help though, is to apologise.

Be someone who says sorry

*****

REFLECT:

Are there times when, with all the best intentions, you over-promise what you can do?

What would it look like to be more honest about the demands you're under and the capability you feel you have in a specific moment?

Think about the power of saying sorry or receiving an apology from someone else. Think about how it can change the atmosphere in a room.

27th February

It's the quiet ones you need to watch. That's what they say isn't it? The noisy ones you know about straight away, but the quiet ones can slip through the net. They're the ones who can go unnoticed if you're not careful, even though they might have just as much anxiety, if not more; just as much 'need' as another child. They just show it in a different way. Or they don't show it at all. Anxiety that peeps above the surface as nail biting and tummy aches, or appearing to 'zone out' in class, might look like something entirely different a few years from now, so seeing it in the 'now' is important.

This morning I was observing little Olivia in class. She's quiet. She goes about her business. She comes to school with everything she needs; listens attentively; always says please and thankyou; makes a start at her work independently; finishes her tasks; likes to do things well; chats quietly with her friend and doesn't need asking to tidy up. But at the start of the day, she struggles to separate from Mum, and in recent weeks it seems to have got worse. Whilst her teacher has already had some conversations with Olivia and Mum, we need to explore it a bit more, because things are just not settling for her. So, once again we open the door to conversation.

Sometimes you just don't know what you're going into. You don't know what's behind the door as you tentatively push it open or ask to come in. Sometimes you knock on the door and there's no reply, and you try again and again, and if you can't get any answer from the knocking you ring the door bell, or call up at the open window or ask a neighbour to pass on a message; sometimes people throw the door wide open straight away and welcome you with a 'Come in!', the relief so loud you feel that everyone can hear it; sometimes the process is more gradual over time; sometimes you're met with a hesitant peep around the corner of the door, with it barely open at all, and that's the way it will stay. . . . But we always need to be people who seek to open doors, so that we can understand more of the person, more of the context, in order to help the child. Our heart is always to approach in such a way as to keep the door open.

Be a door opener

*****

REFLECT:

Think about times when you throw your door wide open to others. Think about when you shrink back and prefer to hide or just poke your head around the corner. How do you feel in both of these scenarios? How could reflecting on this help you think about how you partner with parents?

What kinds of ways do you approach conversations with parents and children? What works best for you and them?

Think about a parent where maybe the door is only slightly ajar. How can you continue to build trust and enhance communication with them?

28th February

One of my jobs today has been to make a start on revising our Bereavement policy. It's something we'll continue to work on as a staff, but I needed to put in some of the legwork first.

Death is a reality that none of us can avoid, and like any other setting, we face bereavement from time to time in our school community. We've had a number of families past and present who have suffered significant loss, sometimes suddenly through a traumatic incident that sends shockwaves out to all who hear the news, and sometimes through the long drawn-out robbing of a life over a protracted period of time. During these times, working alongside other support agencies, we've offered the best support we can. At other times we've lost members of staff and have journeyed together as a school community with our grief. It's a strange thing, grief. It's totally generic, and at the same time totally personal. Universal yet intimate. Shared yet uniquely felt.

A number of our staff have been specifically trained in bereavement and supporting children through grief, but we all have to have a basic understanding of good strategies and language to use around the subject of grief, loss and death. So that's the premise of the policy. It's an uncomfortable thing but we have to be able to look it full in the face. We have to know what we do and why we do it when it rudely interrupts our days.

As I look over what we do, the values we hold, the practices and procedures we have in place, I'm recalling specific children and families and conversations. I'm remembering what they said, what they did, the pictures they drew in the thick of that season. I'm remembering the look in their eyes, the silence and the tears, the questions and the matter-of-fact responses that can sometimes throw you. I'm remembering the way they played or withdrew or acted out.

Considering grief and loss is a holy act of remembering. We are to be full of compassion, sustaining nurturing safe places to recall and remember – creating space for questions and talk, raw emotions and quiet; walking with the wounded and weary, and when the time comes, be whisperers of hope.

Be compassionate

*****

REFLECT:

Think about your own experiences of loss and the impact they've had on you.

How do you show compassion to the children, families and colleagues you work with?

In what ways can you be a whisperer of hope?

Monthly musings

February – Blink and it's gone

It's just a few weeks of the year, but February can be intense because there's so much to fit in, build on and consolidate in such a short time. With a half-term break tucked right in the middle of it, it can easily feel like time is not on your side. But we press on . . .

1 What issues do you currently face around time?
2 How do you go about prioritising what you need to do, should do and want to do?
3 How do you feel when time is not on your side? What pressures does it put you under, and how do they impact on you?
4 Reflect on conversations you've had with parents and carers . . . perhaps where they face timeframes that feel too short or too long. What kinds of pressures do they experience around this and can any additional support be offered?
5 Think about good times and bad times in your role. Why were the good times good, and why were the bad times bad? What did you learn throughout each season?
6 When it comes to upcoming national standardised tests, consider any deadlines for accessing testing arrangements for specific individuals, such as deadlines for requesting adapted reading materials. Are there any children that need to be disapplied from specific assessments? What conversations do you need to be having with parents or carers around these if you've not already done so? Consider the sensitivities around these discussions. How will you plan or prepare for them?
7 Consider the ways in which you measure progress in school. Think about the values that these communicate within your school community.
8 By this half term break you'll be halfway through the school year. How is it going?

9 What do you feel about what you've achieved so far and what you're still working towards?

10 Facilitate a culture of sharing stories with others, to encourage each other along the way. Whilst protecting confidentiality, what story could you share this month with a colleague?

NOTES – My musings . . .

📅 March

1st March

'Morning! Can you just pop in for a minute?' . . . Here we go! After signing in, it's often my first port of call to pop into the school office to discuss staffing needs. Oh, for a week where we don't have to sort staffing cover! It takes so much time, and more often than not these conversations have to happen in some shape or form every single day. Sometimes it feels like piecing together a complex jigsaw puzzle, and it often feels like we're up against it and that time is never on our side.

Sometimes it takes conversations with three or four people just to facilitate releasing one. I need to release so and so to be in on this meeting, which means she can't support this child with physical needs (that are such that he cannot be left without support at that particular time), so I'll ask Mrs . . . to assist with supporting him (because she works with him every afternoon) so he'll know her and she knows him and is aware of his needs and his provision. But in order to release Mrs . . . I need to ask the teacher of the class in which she works if I can please borrow her for that time, and so could she please adjust her planning in such a way that will mean she still gets done what needs to be done in her class . . . and if we're borrowing Mrs . . . that will mean that . . .'s Mum will need to know that she won't be around first thing for a quick touch base re how the morning routine has gone, so I also need to check in with the teacher to make sure she remembers to sort that handover in the morning.

Releasing staff is hard because people are the most valuable resource we have in schools. Time is money and there is no spare money. That means there are no spare people. Like a jigsaw puzzle, there are no spare parts. If one's missing you know they're missing, it affects the overall picture. We have a brilliant staff team who are good at being flexible and finding solutions. It's always about

DOI: 10.4324/9781003333753-8

team-working, being creative and resourcing people, but it's still flippin' hard work fitting the puzzle together.

Be a puzzle-piece finder

*****

 REFLECT:

How does it affect you when you feel like there's a piece missing?

What impact does it have on you and others around you?

How can you create more time and space to find solutions together?

4th March

9.15pm – Googling homemade World Book Day costumes – I don't think I can get away with a duffle coat, hat and pair of wellies again to represent a famous bear. Wearing an all-black ninja-style suit with swag bag in hand, and donning a wig last year gave some of the six-year-olds a fright in my attempt to recreate a thief in the night. It's not that I haven't thought about sorting out my outfit. I've actually been thinking about it a lot. On and off. It's just there have been so many *other* things I've had to think about too. So, it has been very on and off. Well, more off than on, and now I need a costume for tomorrow and I'm cutting it fine.

Call C – hasn't she got a stripey T-shirt I could wear with those trousers? . . . Are you home? Can I swing by and pick it up? It's an 'it'll do' kind of outfit. I don't like that feeling, but that's all I've got time for.

Be creative

*****

 REFLECT:

How do you feel when you feel rushed for time? Or like you've not had the chance to do the very best you wanted to at something?

Sometimes 'it'll do' is enough. How does that sit with you?

Think about all the ways you're creative in your role in school. There are probably loads more ways you flex these skills without even realising because it's just 'what you do'.

5th March

Today I finished gathering everything together to submit a request to the Local Authority for them to assess a child, in the hope that he might be given an EHCP (Education Health and Care Plan), a legal document that details the outcomes we all want for the child, his strengths and needs and the provision that needs to be in place, including the additional money that is needed to make that happen. It's part of the continuing process of working with the parents and the child.

The paperwork requires dedication. There's no place for flippancy or hurry, you work on it *with* the child and parents, *for* the child and parents, making sure you evidence everything required. It's person-centred paperwork put together to present your 'case'. So, the content is paramount, but so is how it looks and how it reads. Maybe I spend more time on it than some, but I figure that it's important. At the end of the day, these documents are about this child, and what he needs. I've jigged the format over the years so that I'm happy it has a good tone and uses the right language. I always include photos so that whoever's desk it lands on is reminded this is about a real live person. Of course it is, that's the point, but I wonder if sometimes when it's the umpteenth bit of paperwork you've looked at that morning, the person doing the reading might sometimes forget the point, or not see the point at all. We all know a big pile of papers can become a daunting something you just have to get through.

The parents are happy with the document and so am I. I've sometimes been told I put too much detail into these kinds of things, but I think the detail is relevant and more importantly that it communicates value to the family. It shows that we've listened, that we know their child, that we've taken time to craft something and that they are worth the effort of the piece and the process. That's the point. That's why I'm conscientious. It can't be careless. So, when I attach all the files and finally press 'send' I feel that I've done a good job. Now it's out of my hands and we wait.

The waiting is frustrating. You never quite know what the outcome is going to be. There's something quite disheartening when you've put your heart and soul into a hefty piece of paperwork to ensure that a child's strengths, needs, provision and progress are genuinely reflected and you know it's being viewed in a room somewhere by people who've never even met the child. How about you just come along and meet him? And I know that this has happened as part of the gathering evidence . . . that someone or some others have come and seen and been with him, but they're not the ones that end up making the decision, they just input their observations and conclusions into the process.

With other kinds of paperwork we submit for different processes, it's even more frustrating if you feel like you've laboured over something and it's just ticked a box for someone else and they've not even taken time to read it properly. That's how it can feel sometimes when you just get some kind of generic 'thank you for your paperwork' reply. You don't feel thanked at all. You just feel like you've been ticked off someone's list.

These bits of paperwork speak about people. They speak of the child and the family. You can't be slapdash or shoddy when it comes to doing your best for children. They're worth far more than that.

Be conscientious

*****

 REFLECT:

Consider a time when you've been described by someone else, but you've felt like you've been misrepresented or that they've not given the full picture. What might you have wanted to say in response?

Think of a situation where you feel like your work has been taken for granted or your efforts have gone unnoticed. How did it make you feel?

How do you get the balance between being conscientious about your work, and yet having the time and energy to do everything that needs to be done? How do you hold that tension?

Think about discussions you have with parents and children. When you record these, how do you convey the value of the person through your content and language?

6th March

Over the years we've had times with children and families who've suffered extreme and sometimes sudden loss through death of a loved one. And sometimes if the bereavement has been anticipated, like after a period of illness, we've seen that child feel anxious when any similar symptom is exhibited in themselves or other people. Of course, you're going to feel worried and may not be able to concentrate and may possibly be overwhelmed to the point of being debilitated if someone even says they have a headache, when headaches accompanied treatment in someone you loved just before they died. They're the kinds of individual details we need to know to support the child in their grief.

When unexpected tragedy comes to a community, there are hundreds of different personal responses within a shared response. In these situations, a sentiment that's sometimes voiced to support children so that they can hold on to some kind of security is to focus on those who are doing the helping. Today as a school community we are experiencing unexpected loss, and as we journey and grieve together, we're pointing our children and families to the helpers and we're being the helpers for each other.

Be someone who points to the helpers

*****

REFLECT:

What kind of supportive relationships do you have within your school community?

How able do you feel to ask for help?

When you've been offered help, how does it feel?

7th March

I came into work today to find hot cross buns in the staffroom. They're one of my favourite things . . . the cinnamon-ny citrus smell, the juicy plump raisins you discover inside, and if you toast them the joy of it all only increases! The giver of the gift was anonymous, but the gift was so valued. It's the little things that put a smile on your face, especially when the pressure's on, and smiles are few and far between. One of the children walked past the staffroom at lunchtime and could smell the treats, the smell wafting down the corridor. 'Ooooh, that smells lovely' she said. Kindness is like that. It lingers in spaces, long after the giver has been and gone. Thankfulness is like that too. They both do something to the mood; they change the air. . . . They're contagious, infectious . . .

Be thankful

*****

REFLECT:

What can you be thankful for today?

How can you show your appreciation to someone else this week?

What do you bring to the atmosphere around you?

8th March

I had an important meeting at 9am today with an external consultant Headteacher, discussing how we were getting along with our action plan around our understanding of children with attachment difficulties and reviewing our provision for them. I'd prepped well for it and had anonymised case studies to discuss, knowing I needed to evidence what we've been doing and why, and planning for our next steps.

As soon as I arrived at school, I realised there was going to be a problem with the arrangements for the day. Sunnie's teacher was absent, and so was another member of support staff in her class, and Sunnie is a child with attachment difficulties. I knew that this would mean her separating from Mum would be particularly tricky this morning. I've been checking in with her for a while now so she knows me well, and I just knew I had to be present for her when she arrived, just to settle her in. She would be upset by familiar staff not being there and would need some kind of security for her to be able to part from Mum and settle into class. But how to be in two places at once? An important meeting and an important child. In discussion with our Deputy Head, I knew I had to arrive late to the meeting and explain why. The Deputy Head could explain my delay, but I had to prioritise the child. This would be a case of demonstrating our understanding of attachment needs in practice, not just talking about it. It's all very well being able to talk to others about what you do, but you have to actually do it.

Greeting children genuinely is so important. It might seem like something trivial to an outsider, but it's the first indicator of consistency and secure relationship that children have as they walk through the door. It communicates that they are known; that you are physically and emotionally present for them; that you are *for* them; that you are pleased to see them; that whatever happened yesterday you are still here for them; that you want the best for them. All these things speak to them about their worth and their place in your school community. Each hello, smile, high five, enquiry about their pet, noticing their new coat or hand on their shoulder as they come in, communicates value to the child. It says this is a safe place. Sometimes we have to choose what's important, and it does well to choose well.

Be someone who knows what to prioritise

*****

REFLECT:

When you feel you have to be in two places at once, how do you prioritise what you do?

Think about times when you know you are known by others. How does it make you feel?

In what ways do you create a sense of belonging for others?

11th March

Here I am again thinking about funerals. Sounds a bit morbid, but today it is apt. Some of our families are grieving, and a funeral is just around the corner. Grief is still that intensely personal, yet strangely collective thing. In your grief, it causes you to reflect, to remember, to evaluate, to thank, to celebrate and everything else in between.

And so I've been thinking . . . I want to make a difference. Not just when I die, but in everyday normal life I want to make a difference. I want people to know that I really cared, and that I did my very best with what I had.

Be a leaver of legacy

*****

REFLECT:

What kind of difference do you think you make to the children and families you work with?

What kind of legacy do you want to leave in your school community?

What do you want to be remembered for?

12th March

Why is it that when you're up against it; when you've got a two-minute window to copy something before a meeting, or before sending some paperwork off somewhere, the photocopier always runs out of paper, or the toner needs replacing!? And then the person you need to ask to replace said toner or allocate said new box of paper is on a phone call and you have to wait, and you just don't have time! Aaargh!! This morning was one of those times where it felt like every second counted.

But then the wondrous beings who are our office staff did what they do every day for me and everyone else, and when they'd finished their call, they fixed what needed fixing and they did it with a smile. If I'd not had to wait, I wouldn't have then been so thankful. Sometimes we're forced into moments of pausing, and in the slowing we're more able to see and be thankful.

Be grateful

*****

? REFLECT:

How does busy-ness affect your day?
What new things might you be able to see if you're forced to pause?
What about if it's not forced upon you but instead you 'choose' to pause?

13th March

On my way through the hall, one of our youngest classes was eating their lunch. I was met with the sight of three newly turned five-year-olds all wearing birthday hats with pretend birthday candles on. Barely able to contain himself one of them called out to me, 'It's my birthday!', so I joined him for a chat. He was whizzing around on his seat, trying to keep sat down but his excitement was fizzing out all over the place. There's an analogy that's sometimes used to describe children who are always 'on the go' . . . that they're a bit like a fizzy drink bottle that's been shaken and all this pent-up energy is just waiting to burst out if the lid is even unscrewed just a tiny bit. Sometimes the analogy is accompanied by a negative undertone, intimating that the child is somehow out of control and needs to be contained. What I saw today was just sheer excitement, brimming over, spilling out. Like the fizz that comes with a popped champagne cork. When you see joy like that it's contagious. It brightens up the room.

Be a celebrator of birthdays

*****

REFLECT:

What interruptions can you choose to celebrate today?

Think about times when you've been so excited you can't contain it. When you tell others about it how does it make you feel?

What kind of language do you use to describe children who are always on the go? What kind of connotations does it have?

14th March

Sometimes there are seasons where the amount of information coming our way feels immense. Sometimes it can feel like every day there's more . . . Updated guidance from Government, the Local Authority, an Academy Trust, health or social care professionals, this organisation, that organisation, these colleagues. Someone somewhere else pings you a document and the work has just left their desk and landed on yours. They have no idea of the impact it will have on your day or week or the coming months as you begin to translate could's and should's, have to's and must's into your school policies and practice. Some days it feels like there's reams of stuff to read and decipher, interpret and digest, do and implement . . . whether that be at a whole school or individual level.

They're all-important pieces of work that need to be done, that need to be thought through, and done thoroughly. They are often things we will be scrutinised on or can't get wrong, and sometimes the volume of it all can feel overwhelming . . . like you're standing under the pouring waters of a waterfall and the water just keeps on coming. Like a drowning. No space to catch your breath. No coming up for air.

That's truthfully how it can sometimes feel.

But we have no choice. We keep going.

Be tenacious

*****

 REFLECT:

How does it affect you when you feel like you're under and you can't catch your breath?

Look back at how you've kept going through difficult seasons. Consider how tenacious you've been.

15th March

Little things matter. Like remembering that Kyle doesn't like his baked beans touching the rest of his dinner. So baked beans on the side in a different compartment of his dinner tray is one solution, or baked beans after he's eaten everything else is another, or sometimes just no baked beans today. Asking him the question is important as well as knowing the facts. Where you put your baked beans may seem like something so small, so insignificant, but to him it's a very a big deal. If we get it wrong, it's not just a case of him 'pulling himself together', or a 'never mind', or a getting annoyed at the scale of his response. He's pretty much in his rights to say, 'I told you so', because he has told us, whether through his words or through us observing his behaviour before. He needs to be met with understanding.

If someone puts marmalade on my toast in the morning, I'm not going to be able to eat it. I like loads of other spreads and jams, but marmalade is not one of them. I might not scream or shout about it, but I can't explain why my reaction is so extreme. I mean, I like oranges, and I like sugar. I just can't do the two of them together. My family know this and so no one puts me through it.

If we know a particular child finds something very difficult or distressing, it's our job, at the very least, to be aware of it. More importantly, we need to act on the information. To adapt our practices. To cater for needs. That means all of us, all of the time. Not as and when we remember, not forgetting to pass a message on to someone who doesn't know. Unintentional mistakes can be made in seconds but the impact on the child can last much longer. If we fail to act, it's our fault not theirs. We're the ones who've failed the child.

Be someone who remembers the everyday things

*****

REFLECT:

How do you feel when someone's forgotten something important about you?

What details that may appear small to others do you know to be important for some of your children?

18th March

Today was a tough day. Sitting with a member of staff who is beside herself; who is 'done'; who feels like she has nothing left to give with a particular child; who is exhausted and has done well just to turn up today after the week she's had so far. It's hard to see a colleague who feels completely spent. It's hard because we care and because we know what it feels like. We've all been there before. Sometimes it's really hard just to keep going.

In schools we have to provide support when people need it. Genuine support, not just lip service. Timely support, not just when it's all a bit too late. Support that's actually going to make a difference. There are times when I've got the timing right and times when I've got it wrong. Times when I've got the support right and times when I've got it wrong.

Sometimes people get to a point where they ask for help. But sometimes they don't, and we need to be skilled at noticing the signs and stepping in. Support can look like a myriad of tried and tested things, or something totally unique to the person and situation . . . It might look like providing some kind of immediate respite or team support, coaching, a space to talk, looking together at planning, provision, practice and strategies, accessing additional support from external agencies. It can be a tweak in practice or a complete overhaul, but the support has to come. People have to know that they have been seen and heard, and that they are not on their own.

Be a reader of the signs

*****

 REFLECT:

What are some of the signs that indicate you might need support?

Think of a time when you needed support. How did the sense of floundering feel?

If you received support, how did it relieve the pressure? What helped?

How can you show support to another colleague this week?

19th March

We have a garden area at school. Not a full-on allotment, but some large planters that children use to grow seeds, care for them and watch their handiwork grow. It's often a slow, labour-intensive process, but something that nurtures care and attention. I caught sight of our eco-team working on it today, getting their hands mucky as they sifted through the soil.

The other day I was in town and from a distance I noticed a young lady about to cross the road. I knew at once that it was a former pupil from school . . . and there she was . . . tall, smiling, and independent in her surroundings. Yes!! I thought.

We don't often get to see the children we've invested in once they leave. We don't often get to see them grow into adulthood, but nevertheless we sow, we water and tend and work the soil, in season and out, knowing that as part of the team around them, if cultivated well, they will bloom.

Be a gardener

*****

 REFLECT:

Think about some of the children and families you've invested in.
How did you invest in them? What did that look like in the day to day?
Now imagine who those children might become.

20th March

The school calendar is ticking, and regardless of what else is on my plate right now the seasonal things that occur in the cycle of school life still somehow need to happen. We're deep into the Spring term and we need to anticipate the significant change that is coming for our children at the end of the school year. Helping children cope with change is a crucial component of developing their resilience. Supporting children around transitions is an important aspect of everyday life in school, but in the summer term we need higher levels of planning around the major changes that are on the horizon.

Transition planning has to be done at all sorts of levels. We have to consider the continuity of what children will learn, their experience of new people and places, the impact of change on their relationships, support for their social and emotional needs, building their confidence and resilience, as well as the administrative handover of information. So, while I'm on my knees, with any notion of a summer break still a way off, I'm letting my mind wander a little, to dream about holidays . . .

When you're getting ready to go on holiday, you prepare. You do your research. If you're lucky enough to be going abroad, you look into the currency, so you can access things when you get there; you look into the climate, so you know what to wear; the different rules (do they drive on the right?), to keep you safe. You check out things to look out for, things to be careful about, where to eat, where to play, what to do, the 'must sees', the 'do's and don'ts'. You might learn a few basic phrases so you can get by. If you've driven on the right before, you're likely to feel a bit more confident in taking to the road and finding your way around. If you're holidaying with family or a travelling companion, it's likely you'll feel more confident than journeying alone; if you're with someone who knows the area and lingo well, then that's an automatic bonus . . . you'll immediately feel more relaxed. You'll quickly gain local knowledge from them, know the best places to eat, to go and the places to avoid. When you have more information, more preparation, more experience, it's easier to settle in.

Just imagine none of these holiday preparations, and you're thrown into a new environment without having had a chance to pack your bags, with no idea of where you're even going, let alone how things work or whether you've got the very basics to survive. We all need time. Time to familiarise ourselves with new routines, places, practices, people, layout, directions . . . you get my drift. You can't hurry transition. So, we talk, and we plan. We think whole class and we think specific children and families. We keep the consistency of presence and routine whilst we introduce changes, we highlight the sense of safety through nurturing relationships even when uncertainty is ahead. We prepare and we keep on right up to the very end.

Be prepared

*****

REFLECT:

Think of a holiday where your preparations went to plan. Compare that to a situation where you felt unprepared. How did the two different scenarios make you feel?

How do you approach change? Is it something you embrace, shy away from or pursue reluctantly?

Identify a child you know who struggles with aspects of change. How can you best support them in the day to day, and when bigger changes are ahead?

21st March

When we can see something's happened, or when it looks like something's gone a bit wrong and a child is unsettled or upset, we say 'I'm here to help'. It's one of our stock phrases in school, borne out of training we've had over the years with a local special school, and today I found myself using it again with a little one who had wedged himself into a corner of the classroom near the coat pegs. The words are not a magic formula, but they open up space to begin a conversation. They communicate that we're not barging in with our own assumptions as to what might have happened, that we're not here to judge or blame, or point the finger or shame, we're here to *help*. Children need to hear that, and some more than others. Sometimes children get themselves into a corner in an emotional sense, and they can't get out. They get stuck . . . and they need a helping hand to wriggle free. Feeling stuck is an uncomfortable thing. You feel hemmed in, unable to move, and you can't see a way out. Some of our most innate responses as human beings are fight, flight and freeze, where our bodies react to situations where we feel under threat. When we see this happen in schools our job is to offer help, to find a remedy, a solution, a way out.

Be someone who offers help

*****

REFLECT:

Think about your own personal responses to situations of perceived threat. What kinds of things do you innately do?

How do you offer help to a child who's got stuck?

22nd March

My friend's husband can't smell or taste a thing. There's some medical reason behind it and it's been like that for as long as she's known him, but it's just today I was reminded of it. It got me thinking about all those experiences you miss out on, when something that is so integrally part of how your body functions, suddenly stops working. I can't imagine what it's like not being able to taste the meal I've just cooked, or not being able to smell bacon sizzling for a weekend brunch. Having one of your senses inhibited or blocked alters your experience of your surroundings. You can adopt different mechanisms and strategies to help and develop other enhanced areas of strength but there still needs to be an awareness that you're experiencing things in a different way to others.

We have several children with hearing impairment at our school, and they are full participants in school life. Our Qualified Teachers of the Deaf bring their expertise to the team and know each child individually; how best to plan for them, teach them and support them, and they share their understanding with us to keep our awareness to the fore. We have to know our children. We have to have the knowledge. It's the responsibility of all of us to put in the work to understand the needs of each child, so that we can give them what they need to thrive in our settings.

Be knowledgeable

*****

 REFLECT:

Consider a child who may experience the world differently to you. Is there a way you can gain more understanding of their world?

Think about training you've had. What have you recently learned that impacts on your day-to-day practice?

Monthly musings

March – Spring is in the air

The anticipation of Spring brings the promise of new hope and new life. Lighter days and pockets of sunshine. Whilst the pressure is on as you hurtle towards ongoing and standardised assessments, the whiff of spring in the air can put a spring in your step as you go about your day-to-day routines.

1 What have you been hoping for during this school year? What do you hope for going forwards?
2 How can you help build a culture of hope with those around you? How can you speak words of hope to your children and parents?
3 Consider anything that is newly happening. What have you been sowing and planting in the lives of your children, families and school community over the year? Where are you are now seeing shoots growing? See these for what they are. The fruits of your labour . . . and be encouraged.
4 Summer testing/exam season is just around the corner. Think about the language you use in school around tests. What culture does it reflect? What values does it convey to children and parents?
5 How can you continue to build resilience in children and parents as they face the 'testing' season?
6 Notice your internal triggers in this 'testing' time. Recognise potential anxiety around you – your own, that of your children and their parents, and that of your colleagues. Have grace for each other.
7 In schools we always strive to see progress, to aim for the best outcomes for our children. . . . Because of the intensity of the process, we are always pushing on and looking forwards, and in so doing, we can sometimes diminish how far we've come.

Consider the progress that has been made so far this year. Help others in your school community to do the same.

8   Some parents will already be starting to think about next academic year and what this might look like for their child. Begin conversations about transition to reassure parents and children that you will plan for this together. Gauge the pace and content of these conversations based on your knowledge of the parents and children. Too much too soon will increase anxiety for some, but too little too late can do the same.

9   Think about your own experiences of change, both positive and negative. What may have surprised you with joy, and what may have interrupted your life with more difficult feelings? What might have been helpful for you during these times? Can you translate any actions that might be helpful to consider in your school community?

10   As you approach the Spring half term break, how will you press into rest and play, to recuperate for the final term ahead?

NOTES – My musings . . .

 *April*

8th April

That didn't feel great. It wasn't great for any of us seeing that child so unsettled, so upset.

So, we look again carefully at what happened. Not just during, but before and after. What was the context? What was the setting? What were the potential triggers? What language was used? What was going on underneath? We ask the questions. We examine the evidence. . . . We look below the surface, like looking below the surface of a pond to the deep water below to see what's lurking beneath. That's how I sometimes view the verb 'to ponder' . . . not just to stay or observe on the surface but to think deeply, to go way down deep.

We need to remember that when we are faced with a situation like this, when we find it hard, it's pretty much always been harder for the child. In that moment of distress, no matter how hard it was for us, it was harder for them, and we need to ponder on that.

Be one who ponders

*****

 DOI: 10.4324/9781003333753-9

REFLECT:

Think again about a situation that didn't go so well for a child. Are there other things you can explore more deeply about it as you continue to reflect?

How do you feel when you come away from a situation where you think you could have handled it better?

How easily are you able to move on from it and start again?

9th April

Schools are amazing places. They are living, breathing, feeling things . . . but if we're not careful, sometimes we can lose sight of the life and the oxygen. When the nuts and bolts of things are all in place and working pretty well, we function, we do all that needs to be done, but if genuine time to gather together and connect face to face is squeezed, things can end up feeling strangely robotic . . . like you can hear the internal workings of a machine. If you're not careful, even though you're surrounded by people, people can start passing each other like ships in the night, everyone on their own agenda with their own to-do-list or functioning well in their own little groups but losing sight of the bigger whole. Losing sight of the people.

It can happen so subtly over time that we don't even notice. We just get caught up in all the things we need to do. But if we see this happening, where's the community? Where's the life? The breath? The blood that courses through veins to keep organs alive in the body, sometimes seems to be replaced by wires and cables, emails and messages, without us even realising. We're functioning, but it doesn't feel like we're together. In individual classes there's the chitter chatter of staff and children, and if you close your eyes, you can be fooled into thinking everything is ok, but sometimes it doesn't feel ok.

In schools we cultivate a sense of belonging, of community and a collective identity, but sometimes if quality interactions with each other are limited it can feel like the whole body is a bit dismembered. We were designed to connect, but instead we feel a kind of dis-connect . . . disjointed. Things that were meant to be joined, jointed, to work together, get rusty. They become dis–jointed. Functions that are performed 'remotely' leave people feeling remote. Even the very word conveys distance, and something of inanimate buttons and levers and systems. It lends itself to component parts feeling isolated. . . .

Today I feel a bit alone in what I'm doing. I'm not, but I feel it . . . and as I feel the soreness of it, the 'on my own'-ness of it, I'm drawn to thinking about those children who often feel isolated and alone; those who often find it difficult to connect, and of how relentless and intense that feeling must be over time.

Be someone who connects others and stays connected

*****

REFLECT:

Are there times when you feel alone or have a sense of disconnect from others? What can you or others do to change this dynamic?

How do you stay connected to your colleagues even in the busy?

How do you build opportunities for connection for the children and families you work with?

10th April

Glitter has this habit of getting everywhere. Anyone who's worked with primary age children will know that. You keep finding specks of it in March and April, on your face, in your hair, well after any Christmas or Diwali festivities have finished. This morning there was still glitter in the air when I met Libby and her Mum.

Libby may be starting with us in September. She is delightful, cheeky, slightly hesitant at first, and she has Cystic Fibrosis. I listen, I ask lots of questions. This will be the first of many conversations so that we can get to know Libby and her family more, as well as learn more about her condition and how it impacts on Libby in her daily life. Maybe the spread of glitter is an analogy that can been used to illustrate contamination or the spread of germs. Granted, bugs don't tend to be sparkly, but they transfer from place to place without you even realising, get stuck on surfaces and show up in the strangest of places. As I start to think about Libby and her medical needs, I realise that this has to be at the forefront of our minds and planning for the foreseeable future. For her, germs that have the potential to get everywhere, and may feel tricky to clean up, have to be kept at bay with strict hygiene measures. We've got a lot to get our heads around, but that's our job.

At the same time, we have to be even more aware of the sense of touch. We need to consider the vast number of touch interactions there are in a day at school . . . the reassuring presence of a hand on a shoulder or crouching down to comfort a distressed child; helping young children cut up their dinner and assisting with self-care routines; children playing with the same toys, picking up the same books, touching the same taps. . . . These are some of the obvious ones, but there is this complex interplay between surfaces, equipment, people and spaces, all of the time. The list is endless, and now with meeting Libby, just as when we consider children with heightened or diminished sensory responses to touch, it is being brought again into sharp focus. With each new arrival to school, each with their own unique offering they bring to our school community, it provides another and continued learning opportunity for us all. It brings a collective growing awareness of the challenges some children face every day.

As a staff team I'd like to think that we have a pretty good awareness of sensory needs and how these impact on some of our pupils. We're used to being flexible about uniform to meet children's sensitivities around clothing – checking and rehearsing the wearing of any costumes in school plays to see if they are comfortable – decreasing the amount of lining up children have to do when moving from place to place, just to minimise any jostling in the line. We're used to having individuals come in or go out slightly earlier to avoid the crowd; having quiet areas for them to go to as part of their daily routine – children wearing ear defenders – altering provision to help limit the overwhelming busy-ness and noise levels of crowded areas. We're used to children having wobble cushions and chewy oral sensory toys. We're used to incorporating sensory breaks into children's days as part of their usual routine. These practices are used day in day out in our school as they are in so many other mainstream schools across the country, but even so, as we learn about Libby, our own senses are currently heightened, and I think that's a good thing. So, let's be alert, not just alert to the germs or risk or danger . . . but alert to sensitivities that impact on our children all the time. Let's look for the glitter in the air.

Be alert

*****

 REFLECT:

Think of a child. What needs do they have? How does that bring the way you look at things into sharp focus?

In what ways do you have to be alert to meet the needs of the children in your class?

Reflect on a child who when you first met them, you knew you had a lot of learning to do about their needs. How did that feel initially . . . and how did that feel over time?

11th April

Today I was watching two children sat by side by side. They were chatting and colouring together during their break. There's nothing remarkable about that in the one sense, but what was remarkable is that I know that one of these children has been going through a tough time and had recently been upset and got angry in class. He'd not got just a little bit angry, but a big kind of angry.

We have to remember that what ultimately drives a child's behaviour is their feelings, and a child's anger is first and foremost their distress. To support children who become emotionally dysregulated, we have to have boundaries and practices in place to help them feel emotionally safe, as well as developing their understanding of consequences and how others can be impacted by their behaviour . . . and what we need to communicate most to all our children is that we are *for* them, and that they have worth, and that sometimes we all need help to feel that way. Sometimes we all have bad days, sometimes we're just scared or overwhelmed.

Children have this amazing way of coming alongside; of understanding others; of getting over things; of embracing differences. They're far better at it than adults. Less things get in the way for them. They make less judgements. They hold less grudges. They don't immediately tend to point the finger or tut out loud. If we can cultivate environments of empathy, we're doing something right. Empathy is the key.

Be passionate about empathy

*****

REFLECT:

How do you support children to move towards being able to self-regulate their emotions?

How do you wipe the slate clean so that a child feels they can start again the next day?

How do you create an environment of empathy?

12th April

There's a train station in London where there's an automatic pre-recorded message that routinely plays to warn passengers to 'mind the gap' between the train and the platform as they disembark. The message plays so regularly that after a while, commuters don't even see the gap anymore, let alone mind it, they just step right over it like it's not even there.

The language of gaps is important. There's always been a lot of talk in SEND around gaps, and the importance of narrowing the gap around achievement and progress for children with additional needs and SEND. There is often a gap when you compare their rate of progress with others. The problem with gaps is that we can know that they're there, like the message that plays repeatedly, but you hear it so often that it just gets filtered out into the background noise of everything else that needs to be done and addressed. Sometimes it can be like you don't even see the gap at all . . . and that's dangerous because it can say something about people's expectations. If we don't have high expectations for the children we work with, we're all in trouble.

Instead, if you tune in and your attention is drawn to the message again and again, you can hear something of its urgency. The message is still being played because the message is still important. It's still something that needs to be noted and acted upon. Do I mind the gap? Yes, I do. I really mind it. I see it and it bothers me, and I along with all of the rest of my colleagues work hard to change it.

Be a mind-er of the gap

*****

 REFLECT:

What really bothers you about meeting the needs of children with SEND? What do you mind?

What frustrations do you feel with wider systems and practices?

What does your data tell you about the progress of your children?

How do you ensure you keep high expectations for the children you work with?

15th April

There's a large number of staff off school today due to illness. A vicious bug doing the rounds. As I step inside the building and realise the scale of things, it kind of feels like a pretty close call to be open at all. So, we go into emergency mode. We're all literally covering everything. No school has spare staff. Budgets don't allow it. Everyone has a specific role (or several) to play . . . there are no spare parts. So today almost feels like an impossible task.

We're all having lunch on the hoof, grabbing a fraction of the time we might ordinarily have if we're lucky, so that we can go and cover a colleague and give them a chance to go to the toilet, support a child with self-care and toileting, supervise in the playground, assist with First Aid, man the phone in the school office. You name it, we're all doing it. All hands on deck. Any planned meetings are now re-jigged, squeezed into other snippets of time or postponed until 'later' when things may feel slightly less chaotic.

But the problem is that this always puts more pressure on, because time is precious for us all. Just as there are no spare staff, there is no spare time in school. 'Later' means you have less days or less time to do what you still need to do. It all still needs to get done. There are deadlines to be met, paperwork that needs to be completed, phone calls that need to be made, and time just feels squeezed. I feel squeezed. Right now, I feel a bit like I'm drowning, just trying to keep my head above water.

The problem is that I want to do a good job. I want to bring my best each day, and today I don't feel like I'm doing that very well. I want to do my best for the people I'm working with, the children, families and my colleagues, and putting things off until later impacts them. It's not just something I can't tick off my to-do-list, it's not yet having the fine details for making that resource that will support that child, it's not being able to reassure that mum about something in a timely way and knowing she will worry and her concern will get bigger and potentially spill out elsewhere, it's not being able to submit that paperwork just yet that will support that child's transition plan.

SEND paperwork and to-do-lists are about people. We have to remember that when it's piled high and the pressure's on to get things completed. We often feel over-run with paperwork, always trying to figure out how it can be more streamlined, so that we have what we need, without well-intentioned but pointless or ill-used extras. But right now, I've got to try to get some kind of balance between wanting to do my best, and just keeping my head above water. So, I'm donning my life-jacket just to keep afloat, and today I'm treading water.

Be a life-jacket wearer

*****

 REFLECT:

When was the last time you felt like you were treading water?

How do you find a balance with all the things you have to do when the pressure is on?

When you have to go into emergency mode and wear multiple hats at one time, how do you then process the accompanying sense of hurry or being overwhelmed when the moment has passed?

16th April

This morning I was with a mum of a child who has multiple needs that impact on his daily life. The family had recently started trialling him on some medication to help around his ADHD (Attention Deficit Hyperactivity Disorder), and she described the effects to me. 'It's like his head and body are going fast like racing cars round a race track all the time . . . and this just slows the cars down a bit'.

Parents often have this way of saying things that makes sense. A way of putting things into words that cuts through the jargon and just says how it is for them. And the beauty is that when you hear something that's just simple, plain and clear, it sticks with you, and you pop it in your toolkit so you've got it for another time when you might need it. There are times when you need to use a different kind of language, like when you're writing reports or applying for funding, but when you don't need to, don't!

Be jargon-free

*****

REFLECT:

Consider the vast amount of jargon that accompanies our roles in school. Think about how exclusive the language is and how restrictive it might be to others who may not know the words and phrases we use.

Reflect on the relief you experience when you feel like you 'speak the same language' as someone else.

In what ways might you need to adapt the language you use in different contexts?

17th April

'What did you do today, Mum?'

Today I was a monster-stomping, shadow-hopping SENCO; a get your sleeves rolled up making mud pies SENCO; a Lego-building, red-brick finding SENCO; a singing songs, tapping rhythm SENCO; a reading stories, word-finding SENCO; a Three, Two, One, eyes on me SENCO; a breathe with me SENCO. . . .

These are my favourite kind of SENCO moments. The golden moments. Where I actually get to be with the children I oversee, rather than just talking about them or writing about them.

Be one who seizes golden moments

*****

REFLECT:

What have been recent golden moments for you?

Why have you recalled those particular moments? What does it say about what you love about your job and why you do what you do?

How does it impact on you when you feel like these kinds of moments are few and far between?

18th April

Today was one of those days that felt overwhelming. Every person in school is responsible for the welfare and safeguarding of our children, and yet some of us are involved more intensely with our school's most vulnerable. Sometimes families cope with a level of stress for a long time, and then there are times or seasons where things become more challenging, and the cracks begin to show.

This morning I felt the weight of my role on my shoulders. You can't always meet with parents face-to-face. It's always my preferred option for all sorts of reasons, like being able to read the room more easily or pick up on nuances of non-verbal communication, so when conversations have to be had by phone these things can be more difficult. With potentially tricky conversations it can feel like every phone call you make you have to listen to all that's being said, how it's being said and all that's *not* being said at the same time. Interpreting the words and the pauses. Reading the room even though you can't see the room.

Sometimes considerations are about gauging how much stress a family is under at a particular moment in time. Of course, it's never just down to me, because any concerns are discussed with or conveyed to safeguarding leads. In school it's all of our business to be alert. There's a whole host of people around, picking up on little things here and there, building up the bigger picture, with eyes open to things that might indicate a level of stress for a family, or increased risk for a child. But it's also true that sometimes we all feel the weight of this thing . . . of ensuring we meet our duty of care. When you're having a conversation over the phone, with no actual 'eyes on', it can feel to some extent like you're on your own, so you're on high alert and super focused. Today just felt like one of those days where it felt heavy, because these are things where we cannot get it wrong, where signs have to be seen. These are the moments that can make headlines that no one wants if anyone gets it wrong.

Be focused

*****

 REFLECT:

What are some of the aspects of your role that can feel heavy?
What support might help you to navigate these times?

19th April

Our link EP (Educational Psychologist) contacted me today saying that several of our parents of children with SEND had commented positively to her about a consultative process we've been going through together as a school. She didn't need to contact me to tell me that, but it meant so much that she did. Because we're busy people, working with other busy people, within busy systems, it's easy to somehow lose sight of the little things when everyone's working at a frantic pace. It's easy to somehow miss people in the clutter of the crowd. Slowing down to say a kind word or making the time to send an encouraging email interrupts people's days with a welcome surprise. When you're working hard it's always a gift to know your time and efforts are appreciated by others.

Be encouraged

*****

 REFLECT:

What things do you think you've done well this week? Don't minimalise them. Be encouraged.

How could you take a moment to slow down to encourage someone else?

22nd April

I referred a child to a specialist local clinic the other week, only to receive a letter today saying that the clinic's funding had been cut and their services are now no longer available. They were hoping that they would be able to continue in some capacity in the future, but it would likely be on a private basis. So now I've got to go back to the parent and say that the support I'd hoped they'd be able to access, might now be trickier to find. It's not right that support services are so scarce, and the ones that are out there are pretty much functioning at full capacity, with excruciatingly long waiting lists. No wonder some families feel like they're swimming against the tide. Recently we made a referral to EWMHS (Emotional Wellbeing and Mental Health Service) for one of our children, and this was declined because the child's needs did not fully meet their criteria. How difficult and potentially dangerous does a child's behaviour have to be before they can access specialised help? It's not EWMHS' fault. It's just at times, the whole system feels broken.

At the end of the day, access to any kind of service comes down to money and capacity. It's the age-old problem of resources. The age-old dilemma that all agencies have to wrestle with.

In schools we do our best with what we have. We make the most of our resources. That's why we're all metaphorical children's TV presenters making elaborate projects out of old toilet rolls and sticky-back plastic. It's why we beg, borrow and steal resources. It's why we're never off duty and we pin ideas on virtual boards and scan the internet for DIY resources. It's why we think outside the box . . . trying to meet children's needs creatively within the resources that we have. So, it's back to the drawing board for this family and this child, trying to think of a way to give them what they need when our number one choice is not available. But we'll come up with a Plan B within the resources that we have. It's what we do.

Be someone who makes the most of what you have

*****

REFLECT:

Think about how resourceful you are and all the ways you strive to do your best for the children and families you work with.

What have been some of your best ideas to meet the needs of the children in your class?

23rd April

We rarely exclude children because it's never the solution. If we do, it always feels like we've failed. We always feel an element of guilt. We always reflect on our practice and ask ourselves what could we have done differently? Where have we gone wrong with provision for this child? What do we need to do now? What are this child's unmet needs? We have to analyse it all.

Sometimes we feel confident in the way we work with children. We know what to do in different situations because we've had experience over the years. But sometimes your confidence can just disappear out of the window in a flash, or you find that it's quietly slipped out the back door without you realising and suddenly you feel like you literally don't know what to do. You feel vulnerable and exposed and ill-equipped for the task.

Sometimes when you work with children with social, emotional and mental health difficulties all the feelings they have about themselves, they somehow project onto you and without realising it you feel completely deskilled, that you're not enough, and stripped of any qualification or sound judgement in the moment. It feels like that's what's happened today. It's debilitating, but it happens, and we have to recognise it when it does, support each other and get to work on changing the dynamic for the child and for us.

Be analytical

*****

 REFLECT:

What are some of your overriding feelings when you work with children who can display difficult or dangerous behaviour?

How do you access support when you feel de-skilled?

How comfortable are you with the process of reflecting on where things may have gone wrong?

24th April

In this job I've come to realise that there are my good intentions, my high hopes, and there's a reality. Sometimes they coincide and I do the things I want to do and hope to do, and at other times there is this mismatch where what I want to do doesn't quite come off or doesn't even get a look in. I guess it's because the scope of the job is so big, and I want to achieve so much for the good of the children and families we work with but balancing what you hope for and what you can actually achieve is an interesting one. It can leave you feeling hopeful and frustrated in the same moment.

I was just thinking about it today . . . hope and frustration. . . . We've got to be honest about these two feelings we carry around. I don't think it's just me that carries them. I'd like to think that anyone who works in a school carries hope and that that's what got them into the job in the first place, but quickly the frustration can come along in some shape or form. It's like balancing scales. Finding the balance. It's always better to have more hope, but if (or maybe when) frustration starts to get heavier we've got to get it out in the open so that it doesn't fester like a bad smell or become a boil that needs lancing. We've got to have safe spaces, safe people where we can be honest and say it how it is. Otherwise, we can all just carry it in secret, and that's where shame can start to eat you alive without you even realising it.

Be honest

*****

REFLECT:

How do you feel when you've not managed to do something you'd hoped?

What do your balancing scales of hope and frustration look like at the moment?

How easy do you find it to be honest about this, and what does being honest about it look like for you?

25th April

I've just come out of an Annual Review meeting. One to be celebrated . . . and I'm beaming! Celebrate out loud! Celebrate together!

Tell each other stories of successes, however big or small. It inspires others and conveys so much of your heart.

Be inspiring

*****

REFLECT:

What inspires you?

What recent successes can you share with others?

How do you feel when there's celebration in the air . . . when everyone recognises effort and perseverance and progress?

26th April

In school, normally parents don't see what other children are doing. They only know how their own child is getting on. They might get snippets of information from their child at the end of the day, or from another parent or child where both parties then try and piece together a bigger picture, but generally as a parent you only know about your child.

But sometimes everything's on show.

Every term we invite parents into their child's class to see how we teach different things, in order to help them support their own child's learning at home. Today it's our Reception classes turn. The difficulty this poses is that all of a sudden everything can feel very public, exposing individual differences, with nowhere to hide. All of a sudden, parents can see how their child and other children respond to the teacher and the lesson. All of a sudden, they have someone else to compare their child to. They can see that their child might not be as good at something as another child; their child might not be able to be as attentive, or to sit as still, or to voice an idea. Their child might not be able to wait for their turn to share their response, or cope with the fact that another child might share the very same idea as them before they do; they might not be able to read as well, write as well. . . . They can quickly notice their child's ability compared to others, and this can feel uncomfortable for some. In the thick of all those feelings, what they might fail to notice is how their child is quick to comfort another child, how their child gets up, brushes themselves off and has another go, or how their child makes a start at something they find difficult, or any number of other things.

In school when we talk with parents, we focus on their child, not others. We focus on their child's learning, their child's progress, their child's achievements, their child's strengths and difficulties, their child's resilience, their child's wellbeing. We are a school that has a long-standing inclusive ethos which is attractive to many; where we value the uniqueness of individuals and all that they bring to the school community . . . but inevitably, because people are people, with their own stories, experiences and feelings, comparison sometimes comes into play, and we all know that comparison can be ugly. More than that, comparison can smother and stifle. It snuffs out confidence and creativity. It does nothing but restrict and inhibit anyone who in that moment feels 'less than'.

So, because we know our parents and children, we talk together beforehand about how these 'parents in' sessions might go. We create flexibility and work together to see how it will work best for them. We try to take the pressure off. In an airport they use the phrase 'excess baggage'. It's the stuff that's over and above what should be carried; the stuff that's extra and brings added weight.

We plan together and try to remove some of the extra weight, the extra pressure for some of our families in these moments.

Even with all the planning, prior conversations and protective measures, I wasn't sure how Elliot or his mum would cope with this morning . . . but it all paid off. They both showed up and got to work together, Elliot was calm and Mum said seeing what he was doing was helpful and she left with a smile on her face.

Be a dispeller of comparison

*****

 REFLECT:

Consider times when you have felt somehow 'less than' or judged by others. Think about the impact this has had on you.

How might some of the children or parents you work with feel this?

Think about some of the adaptations you make on a moment-by-moment basis in order to support children and families you work with. You probably do many of them without even realising, but each conversation and decision conveys care.

Monthly musings

April – Time flies . . .

This is the point in the year where everyone wonders how we got to be here so fast. How is this year two terms in, with only one more to go? How are we ever going to get done everything that still needs to be done?

1 Consider whole class and individual achievements and progress. Reflect on the hard work that you and your colleagues have put in. You will still want there to be more progress but take a moment to think about how far individuals have come.

2 How do you measure different aspects of progress in your setting? Are there some areas of progress that you prefer to record or emphasise than others? What does this say about what you think is important?

3 Look back at what you consider to be specific moments of successes so far. In the busy nature of the job, it's easy to forget these details as you move onto the next thing. Capture them in your mind's eye for a moment.

4 Now is the time for more intense thinking and planning for those transitions that will happen for children at the end of the summer. Implement strategies to support at whole class and individual levels.

5 Identify those children and families who may be potentially more vulnerable during this time due to increasing anxiety about the changes ahead. How can you and your colleagues reassure and steady them at this time?

6 Reflect on your action plans and how things are going. Have you seen an increase in staff confidence and expertise in developing practice and implementing changes?

7 Think about what your key areas of focus will be going forwards into next year.

8 As senior leaders begin to identify where staff will work next year, and with whom, plan the dissemination of this information. What you say, how you say it and the order in which you communicate changes to people conveys a lot about value. Ensure communication is clear and timely.

9 You will already be holding two things in tension – the children who will be leaving you in the summer term, and the beginning of preparations for all those who will be coming to you in September. It's a bit like handing on the baton in a relay race. The baton has to be secured safely before you can move on, but at the same time you're receiving another baton from somewhere else . . .

10 How well do you work with other settings to hand over the relationships you've made within your parent partnership working? How well do you support parents to make the transition as well as children?

NOTES – My musings . . .

 # May

3rd May

Sometimes tiredness creeps in and leads to careless conversation. It was only a little comment, and not even intentional, but my ears pricked up. The problem is that when tiredness is in the mix anything can happen. A few voiced words can quickly accumulate others, gather pace and size and then before you know it there's a full-on avalanche heading someone's way.

We've got to speak about people how we would like to be spoken of ourselves . . . and we have to foster that culture in school even when it feels hard. We have to speak of people highly, and where there are difficulties or problems to work through, do this discretely. The staffroom is a brilliant place to come up with creative solutions, but under stress, if we're not careful, careless words can breed. Words or looks, raised eyebrows or shrugs of the shoulder can be dangerous. We have to be a people who don't write others off, who don't judge, who challenge assumptions, who hold the belief that things can change; that we can work towards something better.

Be someone who works towards the greater good

*****

DOI: 10.4324/9781003333753-10

REFLECT:

How does tiredness impact on you and the way you think and speak of others?

Examine the language you use, and others use when describing the children you work with.

What values do you need, to keep on working towards the greater good?

7th May

I could have cried. In fact, I did have to hold back the tears at the time.

'You are good', I said to her, looking her full in the face . . . this desperate little girl. 'You are good'. Pause. 'You are good'. Pause. In the hope that it would have even the slimmest chance of sinking in.

For all she ever heard was that she wasn't. Shame is a terrible thing. It sticks to people like tar . . . covering them, smothering them, suffocating and silencing their innermost being. Scrape it off, scrape it away, fling it far from here, so that people can enter into the hope of breathing, of speaking, of becoming all they can be.

Be a truth speaker, a life-giver

*****

REFLECT:

Think about words that have been spoken to you that have brought you life. Reflect on what that gave you in that moment and beyond.

Identify children and parents who may experience elements of shame. Where might this occur for them, and how can you counteract these moments?

What if you intentionally plan to regularly speak life-giving words to each child you work with? What could that look like and what might it achieve?

8th May

So, today we had a new delivery of glue sticks. This would ordinarily be a source of great joy that would spread delight and happiness across the staffroom, but today there's the realisation that the ones that have arrived are the cheaper version of the ones we wanted. Not an error in the ordering . . . but a finance-based decision. The good glue sticks are too expensive. The only problem is the cheap ones don't actually stick. You might as well spit your own saliva on the page and see if that works better. Without getting political about it, there is no money in schools . . . and yes, it's not just schools, it's across the board. So I'm not moaning, but it is hard. I know of small schools where if they get information through about a training course, they first check to see if it's FREE – and if it's not, the invitation goes straight in the bin, without even taking a second look. In my mind, that's not ok. What about if they really need that training? And we all need training, because the spectrum of needs we meet daily is wide ranging and ever changing.

There is an increasing number of children in our mainstream schools with additional needs, and many of these include children with highly complex needs, and the resources we have are never enough. We always want to be able to do more. The increase in needs on our doorstep could be for any number of reasons . . . I wonder about a few . . . perhaps incredible advances in medicine mean that children born prematurely are now more likely to survive and thrive where they might not have done so before; children with very complex medical conditions and life-threatening allergies have their needs managed well so that they grow into adulthood. There are complex social factors around poverty, family life and relationships; speech and language development in young children is affected when there is lack of talk in their early years; generational cycles of family breakdown and fragmented families are impacting on children's wellbeing and mental health; levels of anxiety and depression are unprecedented. For all the wonders of the advance of technology, maybe it lends itself to a generation of people who have their mobile phones attached to their hands, with instant access to world issues, and little way of switching off from the constant bombardment of information and opinions. This surely affects our attention spans and our processing of information, and whilst social media is supposed to connect people, perhaps some are becoming increasingly isolated and vulnerable. There are so many things to consider; a huge array of factors that might be at play, but what's clear is that the demands on our schools around providing for children with additional needs and increasingly high-level needs, is only ever going to be on the up.

All this and at the same time, there is such a deficit of resources. In schools we are good at make, do and mend . . . but for inclusion to work at its best, staff have to have the resources to give children what they need. As educational staff we are not trained social workers, or counsellors or psychologists or nurses, yet for many of us we may feel like we take on aspects of these roles within our working days. For many children we need specialist resources and equipment, and for all our children we need high levels of staff expertise. As SENCOs this is one of our challenges as we oversee and develop whole school SEND provision within our settings. But all of us have to speak up. We have to advocate for those in our care . . . and the bottom line is, for children with SEND to receive better than 'make, do and mend' provision, we need the glue sticks we put on the order form.

Be an advocate

*****

 REFLECT:

Consider the variety of needs of the children you work with. Consider what they need.

In what ways do you feel under-resourced? How does this impact on you?

In what ways can you be an advocate for the children and families in your care?

10th May

Resilience is talked about a lot with regards to developing emotional and mental health. It's often referred to as bouncing back, or bouncing forwards from times of adversity or stress, a bit like when a yoyo hits the bottom of the length of its string and has to boing back up with enough oomph to reach your hand. It's about still being able to function during or after a time of crisis. The truth is that sometimes we don't have the oomph, or sometimes we just about do, but we don't feel like we do. Sometimes there's not enough momentum, not enough energy and the yoyo just lags and slows.

The problem is that there's no option for anything else when you work in a school but to be resilient, so regardless of how we feel, we tend to rock up and try to manufacture as much bounce back as we can, whilst trying to help the children and families we work with do the same. We use all the tricks of the trade, all the strategies and resources we can muster up, but we will be doing just that – mustering up, cooking with the leftovers. My yoyo's lagging somewhere way down low.

Be careful

*****

 REFLECT:

How aware are you of when you're starting to lag?

What helps build your resilience?

13th May

The first email I open today is from a SENCO at a neighbouring school, just asking a question. It's a question directed to us all in our SENCO Cluster group. We're a tribe, looking out for each other and supporting each other. Sometimes you feel like you've been thrown in at the deep end as a SENCO. It certainly feels like that when you first start. You step into the role, and whilst you'll likely have some SEND training and experiences from being a teacher, the SENCO qualification helps you to think like a SENCO but doesn't really prepare you at all for the daily nuts and bolts of the job.

You don't know where or how to refer families to different agencies – what forms need to be completed for different processes, who the best person is to speak to about this or that; the various timelines you have to adhere to, all the different acronyms and abbreviations that are batted around, Local Authority or Academy Trust logistics etc. If you're a teacher or an LSA you have similar experiences, just maybe without the SENCO hat on. There are always lots of things to get your head around, new systems to become acquainted with, new strategies to implement. Whatever role you have in school, when you're meeting the additional needs of children, other colleagues are a lifeline. You suddenly remember that you're not on your own, and that we're all playing the same kinds of roles in different settings, but with similar challenges.

Be part of a tribe

*****

REFLECT:

Think back to when you first started working in a school setting. Reflect on how much you've learned.

How does your role differ from how you first imagined it to be?

What different groups are you connected with that provide support? Are there ways this could be enhanced?

14th May

Another day, another sensitive conversation. Jack's mum has requested a place for him at Breakfast Club. We know it's important for him to have a settled start to the day, and we know that she needs some wrap-around care, but in order for him to be settled in that provision he's going to need some additional support, not just in the form of visuals or strategies, but in the form of a person, at least to start off with, so that he settles – but quite possibly some support may need to be ongoing because of the complexity of his needs. He has funding to access additional support during other periods of the school day, but if he now also needs support before school starts that might well mean taking some away from somewhere else, because we won't be given any more money. We think creatively when it comes to funding, provision-mapping and support. We have to because there's never enough money to do everything you really want to do.

So, one small request from Mum now requires a lot of thinking. We feel passionate that he's entitled to access the same 'before school' provision as everyone else, but the sums don't quite add up. When we regularly review our SEND provision, one of the things we think about is how well children with SEND can access every part of school life, and this inevitably includes their inclusion in extra-curricular activities and clubs. We have an inclusive ethos as a school, and so we bend over backwards to try to make it happen. We do risk assessments, we think hard and plan carefully. Sometimes it feels frustrating that people don't really see the effort and time we put in behind the scenes, just to make something happen. It's not that people don't appreciate it. It's just they don't fully know what it's taken to achieve it. So, we'll do our best to make this happen, even if at this point, we're not quite sure how.

Be someone who makes things happen

*****

 REFLECT:

Reflect on how important it is to feel included. Are there situations where you have felt the opposite, and how has that impacted on you?

How do you create a sense of belonging in your school community?

When you're faced with a dilemma where you want to make something happen but are not sure how, how do you go about exploring the options available?

15th May

The tiredness feels relentless. I got in from work today, went through the usual routine, changed into non-work clothes and then sat down briefly with a cup of tea . . . except the sitting down became not so brief, as I soon dozed off. School's only been back a few weeks, and I'm already shattered. How is that possible? How is it that I can feel so tired in such a short space of time and with so long to go?! When I came round (and 'came round' it was, because I felt like I'd been knocked out), I tried to conjure up some kind of energy to think about getting dinner ready, and quickly realised that the meal I'd planned actually takes that bit more preparation time than the time I now had. So, I needed to come up with a different plan, but my brain still felt like fudge. Fortunately for me, middle child came to the rescue, and rustled up a tasty dinner for us all. I'm fully aware that's a luxury some families don't have, but I am truly thankful.

Be thankful when others share the load

*****

 REFLECT:

Who do you have that supports you when your resources are running low?
Do you need to develop or expand your support network in some way?
How well are you able to acknowledge when you're tired?

16th May

7.00am

I must catch Laila's mum at the start of the day. I might be called upon to do a hundred and one other things the moment I set my foot in the door, but I must catch Laila's mum.

Be intentional

*****

 ## REFLECT:

How well do you manage to stick to your intentions?

What are you going to be intentional about this week?

Our intentions shed light on our convictions, values and priorities. What do you consider to be the most important thing for you to hold onto today?

17th May

Today I did a lot of reading. A lot of hard reading. Reading the detail. Reading in between the lines. Reading some words and phrases that I had to look up what they meant. Sometimes I call it 'government' reading. It's reading with vast numbers of chapters and headings and sub-headings. If you've been in education for a while you'll have seen waves of new ideas, theories and strategies come along over the years. Some stick around for a while and become an integral part of practice, and others seem to come and go on a whim, with no more permanency than a feather on a passing breeze. Sometimes new legislation or guidance is exhausting to read. It takes time and effort to properly read and understand what's been issued . . . what we *must* do, what we *should* do, as well as try to translate the information into our context, our school, with our particular children and families, our building and resources. When the pace of change is fast and new systems have to be implemented quickly or occasionally what seems like overnight, or when the extent of upcoming change feels overwhelming, it gets me wondering if this might be a glimpse of how some children feel when faced with new information and constant changes in any 'normal' school day.

We're all just trying to make sense of the world around us, and when that world or the information about it keeps changing, it's unnerving. Multiply that feeling for some children who struggle with processing information. Information and change that we might not even consider to be new may be full-blown things that they need more time to absorb and adapt to. In situations where it's information overload, where things are seemingly sprung upon us or where there's little certainty about what's ahead today or tomorrow, let alone the future beyond, it can be unsettling, or anxiety-inducing. We might try to put a brave face on it, or just soldier on with what needs to be done, but it's a fearsome thing to stop and look something straight in the eye and feel like you're not in control.

What if these are similar feelings to those some children feel on a daily basis? If we linger in these places, if we feel the brain fog, if we allow ourselves to feel the discomfort rather than try to sweep it away, maybe it can help us consider more fully the planning and attention needed to support children.

Be a lingerer

*****

REFLECT:

How do you approach assimilating new information and putting it into practice?

How does your capacity for it differ if it's something that interests you or if it's something you just 'have' to do?

Identify a child for whom information overload and processing information is particularly difficult. How are they supported in this process?

20th May

I was in a cluster meeting today of fellow professionals from other local schools, and one of our tasks was to review some of our action plans and our progress towards each step.

Action plans are just that . . . a call to action. It's not a case of calling us out of *in*action. It's not like we weren't doing anything beforehand, but it's just now there's an additional focus, or a pressing need to address, a certain something we need to develop or improve, all with the view of better outcomes for children. The other things we're doing haven't gone away. They're still very much there, it's just now there are other things to think about too. The thing with action plans is that they have to inspire, they have to move things forward . . . and if we're the ones driving the momentum within our settings, they have to capture our personal attention and heart. They can't *just* be a mind thing. Mind things work to an extent but doing things dryly doesn't tend to catch on. If we *believe* in what we're doing and why we're doing it, it makes all the difference to us and to others.

But the tricky bit is balance. Action plans are all about aspiration and casting vision, whilst recognising where we're at now, and that has to include recognising our capacity. It's just I'm not sure we're always very good at that in education, because we always need to be doing more. There's never a season of rest, or to just keep doing what you're doing. The drive is always for better. It comes from the powers that be, whichever government is in power, and so with our striving for better, better, best, somehow our capacity is supposed to be endless, never-ending, almost immortal. When we're working collaboratively on action plans the question that also has to be asked is what reserves and resources do we have to pull this thing off? What is a realistic timescale for change, or for each next step? Sometimes this bit can get lost in the excitement or demand of the new or developing thing, and then we're in danger of biting off more than we can chew, or being unable to digest the new diet, which just leaves everyone feeling bloated and uncomfortable like you've eaten too much.

But when we get it right, when our plans are crafted well, there's a buzz. When plans enthuse and are owned by everyone, it's like the ingredients come together and finally you all get to enjoy a slap-up meal at the end of your labour. Action plans are great. We just really need to bear in mind where we're at and take one step at a time. That's how you follow a recipe. You can't just skip to the end to get to the meal.

Be mindful

*****

REFLECT:

How do you help communicate vision to others around developing SEND provision?

Is your heart behind your action plans?

How well paced are your plans? Are they aspirational and yet realistic, or does this aspect of them need reviewing?

21st May

The wheels feel like they're falling off a bit; the cracks feel like they're beginning to show. When it comes to resilience and bouncing forwards when you've been knocked down, there doesn't feel like there's much 'bounce' around at the moment. We're all exhausted. Shattered. Like things feel when they're pretty broken. The usual exhaustion I feel at the end of June I'm somehow feeling now, and the thought of making it to the end of the summer term seems somewhat overwhelming. It's a running joke with the family that I don't need to be in on the decision-making about what film we might watch on TV, because I'll be asleep on the sofa within the first half hour. We're seeing the fatigue with staff and with parents, where people have held things together for most of the year, but now everyone's resources are petering out, things are just a bit fractious and there's less grace around.

It's timely that we're delivering training on emotional wellbeing these next few days. We use the analogy of putting your oxygen mask on yourself before helping others, but as I'm preparing it today, I desperately don't want it to feel like just lip-service; like we're just ticking a box because that's what we're supposed to do. I want it to be something where people feel invested in; something that communicates value; a space that creates opportunities for people to talk, reflect, problem-solve and find tools that will bring some kind of ease, relief and comfort over time. We just need some space and some grace. We're trying to facilitate us all keeping well.

Be a wellbeing facilitator

*****

 REFLECT:

How in need of oxygen are you right now?

What does staff wellbeing support currently consist of in your setting?

How might you be able to create greater space and facilitate greater grace to explore wellbeing needs more effectively?

Monthly musings

May – Dig down deep

You've come so far but there's still such a long way to go. You may feel that you don't have sufficient resources for the road that's left ahead. So this is a time to dig down deep.

1 You will have all sorts of deadlines looming and looking too far ahead can sometimes feel overwhelming. Keep on keeping on, one task at a time, one step at a time, one day at a time.

2 Remember to communicate the importance of balance. Standardised national tests only give a small part of information about a child. You will have far more knowledge of other areas of achievement and progress that also need to be conveyed to parents this term. How will you go about doing that?

3 If you've not already started to, you'll soon be in the thick of writing end of year reports for specific children, for them to give to their parents. Include real detail about the child that lets parents know that you *really* know them – about their efforts, attributes and character, as well as their progress. What would you want to read, and how would you want things to be said if you were on the receiving end of your report? Be truthful, but carefully consider the language and tone you use.

4 How well do you incorporate child and parent views, not only in your end of year reporting, but throughout the year? Is the collaborative process of working with parents and children reflected in your paperwork?

5 How creative are you in gathering children's views? Do you ensure that all children have a voice and means to express their views?

6 Think back to your own personal school reports. What did they have to say about you? Were they an accurate reflection of who you were at the time? Did they describe your achievements well? If your former teachers could see you now, what would you like to say to them?

7 Think about the format of your reporting. Does one size fit all? Or might you need to change the format for some individuals to make it a more relevant way of communicating their achievements?

8 Audit your current provision and resources. Where might you need to develop your provision and resources going forwards?

9 Consider how you and your colleagues feel when you are able to deliver the provision you know your children need. When this is more challenging how does this impact on your self-confidence?

10 As you reflect on and summarise your achievements this year at a variety of different levels, how do you feel? How do those feelings impact on how you press into the last remaining weeks of the year?

NOTES – My musings . . .

 June

10th June

Today felt like a game of answerphone ping pong all day. Aaargh!!
I just wanted answers to different questions, and I wanted the
answers quickly, because that would mean I could get on with the
next thing . . . but no one was around, so instead, I've had to put
those things on hold until another time. It's just sometimes you feel
like you haven't got the time or space to come back to something.
Sometimes you've got the momentum and you're 'in the zone', and
you won't quite be in the same zone when you come back to it
tomorrow.

I followed up all my requests and questions with emails, but that
means I now have to wait for a response, whereas what I'd really
wanted was just to speak to someone straight away. I'm frustrated
that I can't get done all I'd wanted to, but the questions need
answering so I'll be back to trying again tomorrow.

Be someone who tries again . . . (and again . . . and again!)

*****

DOI: 10.4324/9781003333753-11

REFLECT:

How do you feel when you can't complete what you'd wanted to?

When you have to go back to something, how do you create the capacity to keep on trying?

Think for a moment about parents who have to liaise with lots of different agencies and professionals about their children, and the frustration they might feel on a regular basis when they can't get the answers they're looking for.

11th June

Sports Day. Sun hats and water bottles . . . tick. Rehearsed events . . . tick. Sunshine . . . tick. Photographer . . . tick. Events have been rehearsed, there's cheering and shouts of encouragement, and the school field is heaving with parents, carers and grandparents, aunties and uncles – families giving their all, relishing in the achievements of their children. For some children this is where they really shine. They might not be great at the more academic side of things, but they have a natural athleticism or practised grit and determination, and you can literally see their confidence bursting out as soon as they put on their plimsolls. For others, this is where their achievements fill those 'in the know' with expansive pride, even though others may be oblivious to any achievement at all.

But there's also FOMO. It's a thing, right? Fear Of Missing Out. We've all had times where we've missed out, where for some unforeseen or dreaded reason we've had to forego a party or anticipated celebration. Sports Days are celebration days. Like other school events they're far more than just the content of the programme. They're about being together. They're about family. They're about belonging, and identity and community all rolled into one. They're places where no one should miss out. Today several of us worked hard to support a little one who's Mum couldn't come because she was ill. Sometimes family don't come for other reasons, and there are gaps to fill. No matter how hard you try, no matter how many cheers you give you can't quite undo the fact that mum couldn't make it on the day. You can make it a bit easier with your encouragement, reassurance and smiles, but sometimes you just have to acknowledge that it might well still feel to them like they somehow missed out. It's a hard thing to watch.

Be together. Be community

*****

 REFLECT:

Think of a time when you missed out on something. Remember how it felt at the time.

What kinds of things do you do to ensure children and families don't miss out?

How do you create togetherness and community in your setting?

17th June

Today I cried. Not just a little bit – but full-on sobbing. I am totally exhausted. It's nearing the end of term and whilst some might say staff are starting to wind down at this point . . . (to whom I would say, really?! Have you actually ever met anybody who works in a real-life school?!) As SENCOs, our workload is not just still going full pelt but has been going at break-neck speed throughout the summer term, with us working hard to make children's transitions and transfers to new settings as smooth as possible.

Children leaving us and children coming in, children moving to different year groups . . . so much to do, and so many people to liaise with to give these children the best possible start. I cried because we'd requested short term funding for several children to help support their transition to their new setting, but due to the current context of funding where you have to jump through what seems like endless hoops to even get a glimpse of some money, some of our requests have been declined. Good practice and legislation emphasise the importance of early intervention. It's not rocket science. You give children intervention where and when they need it, and for some, the challenges are minimised, or even totally solved. But if those who need far more cannot access it when they need it, things can escalate, increase, multiply . . . whatever word you want to use. At the end of the day, it's simple maths. There is not enough money where it's needed, and when you know a child will benefit from targeted support so much but you're not in a position to be able to give them what they need, it feels just plain wrong, and it goes against your job description. So, today was hard, but if it takes blood, sweat and more tears, we'll try again, and keep on trying, in the hope that the children who need more, get more.

Be persistent

*****

REFLECT:

Consider the persistence you show time and time again in your work with children and families.

Can you think of a time where you felt a sense of injustice around a child's needs not being met in the way you'd hoped?

What does this say about your values?

18th June

Much of my job is to work with others to problem-solve things ... situations, logistics, resources, strategy, ethos, conflict resolution etc. Trying to unstick things where things feel stuck; trying to see things from a different perspective and look at alternative possibilities. Sometimes it can feel like a really hard number puzzle, or a crossword where the clues feel so cryptic, you're not even sure where to start, yet we put our hearts and minds to the task.

But sometimes we just need to listen and *not* try to fix things. Some situations can't be fixed. Even with the best working together with others, sometimes there are limited solutions. Sometimes what's going on is a bit bigger; sometimes the wider systems feel just a bit too stretched or broken to be able to make a real difference. I know that all sounds a bit doom and gloom, but it can feel like a very true reality at times.

I was listening to a Mum today who just felt like she needed to fight for her child. She wasn't cross with us, but she trusted me enough to be able to let it all out. She was so frustrated with some of the external systems around funding and resources and access to services. She was just so tired of always having to 'evidence' what she and her family experience every day. As if she's before a judge and a panel of jurors, who somehow examine the documentation, the eye-witness accounts, and make a considered decision . . . a decision that means little to them yet means everything to the family in question. She was so tired of the endless forms to fill out; the waiting; the often-poor communication or lack of information that needs to be chased; the sometimes feeling 'done to' rather than being an integral part of the discussion where her voice feels heard and valued. For all the doing and all the problem-solving, sometimes we just need to listen in order to be trusted.

Be trusted

*****

REFLECT:

How would you respond if you felt like you had no voice or that what you said had to be evidenced all the time?

Consider how this might feel for some of the families you work with.

In your setting, how do you develop trust in relationships with parents, carers, and family members?

19th June

Today has been a day of aches and pains. Two colleagues returned from the weekend having sustained injuries from sporting activities, so they're slightly incapacitated, and a number of others are off with a virus. It feels a bit like we're all having to work with one hand strapped behind our backs. Not all of us are fully functioning.

In schools each of us have a specific role to play. We bring different skills to the fore, but we work together, much like the interlinking parts of a body, and when we're all working at full strength, we work in the way in which we were designed, and it all works. Today it feels like we're not at full strength at all – we're carrying injury. We're stretched, and there's a sense that you can only stretch something so far before it snaps.

If parts of a body are impaired in some way, sometimes other parts or senses can become enhanced and more finely attuned to the situation or change in the environment, so that the body can still fully function. So it is with schools. In the short-term, it has its benefits. Our perspective shifts. It means people become more aware of what's going on elsewhere in school. They step in. We help each other out. We see the tension and discomfort elsewhere and we share the load.

But on the other hand, sometimes when there is impairment, other parts of the body can compensate, and by just trying to keep going, we sometimes inadvertently cause secondary damage. I think back to times when I've twisted my back or neck, and whilst trying to protect myself from the pain, I've found myself tensing up and moving more awkwardly, ending up with aches elsewhere because of the adjustments I've tried to make. If the body is impaired, and we find ourselves trying to compensate for sustained periods of time, this lends itself to stress and long-term injury if unnoticed or undiagnosed. I guess at these times what we want is for the strain to be noticed, or at least for it not to go unnoticed. So, right now, we're all being flexible, and doing our very best to take the strain, but I do wonder how sustainable it all is. I do sometimes wonder about the long-term impact on staff wellbeing and everyone's physical and mental health. We're plugging the gaps for now, but we haven't got unlimited capacity or resources.

Be flexible, but notice the strain

*****

REFLECT:

How aware are you of pinch points others might currently be experiencing in your setting?

When you step in to support, how do you respond if it feels like this is not fully appreciated by others?

Monthly musings

June – Summer fun

In the summer months, rather than slowing down in any way, schools often make time for lots of extras. Sports Days, school trips, celebration events . . . extra activities that enhance everyone's experience of the school community. With the extras comes a lot of additional planning and preparation.

1 As you plan and go on school trips or engage in other additional summer whole school activities what do you want your children not just to learn, but to experience? What do you want them to feel? What do you want them to remember?
2 Recall any school trips or special events you had in your own schooling. Why do you remember these particular ones?
3 Think about the school trips you go on. How creative are you with what you offer your children? How accessible are these experiences to everyone? Do you always stick to a tried and tested formula, or is there room to think about the specific needs of your cohort?
4 How do your summer activities reflect inclusion and develop a culture of belonging?
5 Choose one child you work with. Reflect on their school year together with them, like 'a year in the life of . . .' Are there ways in which this conversation then sheds light on what they have experienced? Does it highlight any differences of perspective, or lead you to explore any assumptions you might have made about their experiences? How might this inform your practice going forwards?
6 Consider the relationships you have built and the ways you have invested in parents and carers this year. What has worked well? How has this impacted on parent confidence and the parental experience of being a part of your school community? Where might you still need to develop parent partnership in your setting?

7   How well have you worked with your colleagues this year? What obstacles have you had to work through? What might this have taught you?

8   Continue to recount your successes as you look back over this past year. About what have you been particularly pleased? Have there been any surprises, and in what ways did they surprise you?

9   As you prepare for new children to come into your school and current children to move on to new settings, ask those around you for a few key words to describe your setting. Ask children and parents. Use these to create a word cloud, where the most frequently mentioned words are written in larger font-sizes. What does this information tell you about people's experiences of your setting? Are your values being communicated clearly in practice? If you ask the same of your colleagues where might there be similarities or possible differences?

10   What do you personally want to achieve next year?

NOTES – My musings . . .

 # July

2nd July

This morning saw the end of year show for our oldest children, and as usual, there's not a dry eye in the house. We reflect on how they've grown, what they've achieved, how they've persevered, the shared joys and the shared pain. The best bit for me? Seeing little Morgan hula hooping his heart out . . . and catching a glance at his Mum – So much pride!

Be proud

*****

 REFLECT:

When you think about the progress various children have made, what's your overriding feeling?

What brings you pride when you reflect on this past year?

Aside from core subjects, in what ways have children excelled or made progress this year?

DOI: 10.4324/9781003333753-12

3rd July

By mid-morning I'd had enough. Poring over information about progress pictures and termly attainment. I have a confession to make. I hate data. I mean, I really loathe it . . . and yet, in my role I have to use it all the time. Yes, I know there are different kinds for different purposes . . . quantitative and qualitative, hard and soft, and I have to be good at gathering it, analysing it and using it to inform future practice. I know that all the figures, percentages and graphs represent the children themselves, but the problem I have is that I think people can lose sight of this so quickly. Yes, trends reflect what's going well or not so well, and that's important . . . but each one of those dots or points on a graph is a person with their own backstory, their own context, their own life events happening as we speak, which don't necessarily show up when they're plotted onto paper.

There's something quite 'final' that occurs when you're entered into a graph or table. . . . At that point in time, this is what you were, this is what you achieved and there's no swaying from the evidence. But as people, we're far more 'alive' than that. We have good days and bad days, and life doesn't stand still around us. It's a bit like each child's life being a huge painting on a canvas, but if we're not careful we just zoom in and scrutinise a few paint strokes, analysing their colour, and tone, without panning out to see the picture as a whole, with all its depth and perspective and master strokes. Always give the bigger picture. Not as an excuse, but as an explanation. Always breathe life into facts and figures. Always tell the story.

Be a storyteller

*****

REFLECT:

Think back to your own school days and any results or school reports you received. How accurate a description were they of you then, and what about now?

Consider the story of a child you work with. Think about how you capture it as fully as possible when you record their progress. How do you choose what's important to tell?

4th July

Toner's out again!!!!!!

Be exasperated/patient*

*(*delete as appropriate)*

*****

REFLECT:

What small things make a big difference in your day-to-day role?

Where could there be tweaks to the way things are done to make things run a little smoother?

How do you feel when something apparently so small gets in the way of the bigger things you have to get done?

How can you relate this to how parents may feel when 'technical' difficulties in wider systems and processes sometimes get in the way of them receiving information or seeing processes completed?

5th July

No time to write. Just turning up and getting on with it all. Day after day. Hanging in there.

Be a turner-upper, a show-er-upper

*****

REFLECT:

What are your resources like at this point in the term?

How do you feel about times when you just turn up and show up?

How do you feel when your enough is maybe not your best, but it is enough?

10th July

Today I got an email from a parent of a child who left our school last year to move onto a local Junior School. It was out of the blue, and we've had no correspondence for a year, so it was a total surprise. She simply said thank you. It was like a congratulations. A thank you for all the hard work we put in, for the conversations which opened up questions and for the working together to try to figure out what was going on for him. Now he has just been given a diagnosis and although that doesn't change the provision in place for him (because school were providing what he needed anyway), his mum said it reassured her and helped her to explain to others more about him. Sometimes we don't see the fruit of our conversations. Sometimes these come long after our involvement with a child or family has finished. But the investment is always worth it.

Be congratulated

*****

REFLECT:

If you could go back and say thank you to someone from your own school days, who would it be and why?

Think about a child or family that you have invested in. Even if you didn't see it at the time, imagine the fruit you hope it will bear. How does that make you feel?

12th July

I feel completely spent, but there's no let up. I can't seem to focus on the paperwork I have to do, even when I get a chance to do it. Every task feels like something I have to wade through. Even the usual tasks feel harder. Physical, mental and emotional resources are low.

Four things happened last week that showed me how I'm doing. On Monday I woke feeling so nauseous I was going to vomit. After ringing into school to say I wouldn't be in, I slept for hours as my body tried to recuperate. On Wednesday I went to do a supermarket shop, getting the shopping for my Mum and Dad to drop off later at theirs in the week. Everything was going so well. I was almost congratulating myself that I'd managed to get everything off the list and get through the checkout, drop the shopping off home before heading out again to collect my daughter from work, only to find that my bank card was missing. Panic ensued, along with the emptying of shopping bags, checking pockets, retracing steps and then returning to the shop to find I'd left my card in the checkout card machine and the cashier had kept it safe. I have *never* done that before, and it's surely a sign of being doggone tired.

On Thursday, I opened my emails to read a fairly abrupt reply from an external source querying why we were re-requesting some temporary funding to support a child. The email was followed the next day by another one in the form of an apology, saying that the first had been sent based on some misinformation, but on reading the original email it had already tipped me over the edge. I made my way to the staff toilet and literally sobbed. Not little whimpers, but the big sobs that you hope no-one else can hear; the ones that rise up from your gut. I'm just so tired. And I feel almost guilty saying it out loud, because so many of us are feeling at the end of ourselves. It's just been a long, hard term, and we feel pretty done.

I'm tired of something else always being added to my to-do list when I'd thought I'd crossed something off it; tired of having to jump through so many hoops to get funding for children who need it. It feels like it's only getting harder. No wonder parents feel like they always have to fight. It feels like that for us right now. And then today, Friday, I dropped the shopping off to Mum and Dad's and stayed for a quick cuppa and then I left, with just enough time to go and collect our eldest daughter again from work. Ten minutes into my drive home I realise I've not got my bag or my phone, and that I must have left them at Mum's. None of those things are very earth shattering, but I know that for me, they're a sign that I'm tired, and I'm trying to read the signs. I'm so very tired, and at the moment, summoning up the resources to face each day feels like a big deal. So, in order to preserve my sanity and my health, my to-do list can sit and wait this weekend, because I need to rest if I'm going to make it to the end of term.

Be aware of how you're doing

*****

REFLECT:

How are you doing?

How good are you at resting when your body says you need to?

18th July – Two days until the end of term!

My phone rang this morning, with my colleague in the office asking me to go to a class because someone had something to give me. The tone of the message sounded like I was wanted straight away so I left what I was doing and as I knocked on the classroom door I was met by Taylor, one of our older children who will be leaving to go the Juniors at the end of term. Taylor presented me with a gift. I responded with a thankyou and commented on how smart he looked in his party outfit, and after thinking a while he responded with a compliment of his own. And it was so innocent and so lovely, and then the conversation continued.

He talked about how he was feeling about leaving and going somewhere new. 'A bit nervous' he said hesitantly, and we talked about how he felt when he first arrived with us, but now look how at home he feels! We talked about what he's enjoyed in school, what have been his highlights, the friendships he's made, his favourite books. And I don't want the conversation to end because this conversation does something to my soul.

Because before me is a child with a back-story that I know, a child who every day shows remarkable resilience, a child I have had the privilege of sharing time with, of vulnerable conversations with his mum around the trauma he has faced multiple times over. And here he is standing before me, and he is a joy. And this interaction will remain with me for a good while to come. This interaction itself is the gift. Worth far more than the chosen present he has just placed in my hands, lovely though it is. There are moments that you cherish. Unexpected gifts that come out of the blue that stay with you if you don't rush on to the next thing, and I've decided I'm going to let this one linger.

Be a receiver of the unexpected

*****

 REFLECT:

Consider experiences you've had like this . . . where you receive something unexpected and deep joy takes you by surprise. Think about how this impacts on you in the moment as well as afterwards.

Think about the back stories you know of children you work with. Reflect on the resilience that some children show just coming to school each day.

19th July

SCHOOLS OUT FOR SUMMER!!!!

I love my job . . . but this is the *best* day of the year, because by this point, we're on our knees. By this point I've been religiously taking Vitamin C effervescent tablets every day for the last few weeks. I can feel the sniffles in my nose, and I've been trying to stave off one of my giant cold sores. My family have this running joke that by the time the summer holidays come I'm usually sporting a cold sore that seems to take on the shape of the place where I'm going to be holidaying. I've sported cold sore scabs that look like Cornwall, as well as Wales in the past, and all sorts of other places in between. So, the last day is the best day, the Anticipation-Of-Rest Day. Five or six blissful weeks. Yes, there'll still be work to do, and planning to plan, and emails to answer, but oh, the books I can read! oh, the films I can watch! oh, the wine I can drink! oh, the friends I can see!

Admittedly in weeks one and two I'll just be trying to recover. Being able to sit down on the sofa without falling asleep at the drop of a hat tends to happen about week three. Doing anything before that doesn't stand a chance. And if you get away without being ill at all, it's a result. But hey, I'm not moaning. Schools out for summer!

Be relieved

*****

REFLECT:

Well done. You have been the bringer of your enough.

And breathe. . . .

Monthly musings

July – Approaching the year end

Nearly there. It always feels like there are so many loose ends to tie up before the end of term. But whilst we can be distracted with all that there is to squeeze in, it's also a time where we need to be emotionally present. It's a time of goodbyes and moving on.

1 Reflect on endings you've experienced personally. How did they impact you? Were they done well? If you could go about them differently, what would you change and why?

2 Who was your favourite teacher when you were at school and why? What was it about them that influenced you?

3 Consider the kinds of loss children have to face on a regular basis. How do you support children to journey through it and build their resilience?

4 How do you prepare for change? Do you embrace it or try to avoid it? Think about the feelings you experience as you anticipate change.

5 Encourage children to identify both similarities and differences as they anticipate moving from one setting to another, or one class to another.

6 Don't underestimate transitions that you may perceive to be 'small'. Consider the impact of these on specific children.

7 Get as many class-based and individual resources as possible ready now for September, because even though you may be tired, the importance of these resources, on the back of recent transition conversations, is currently fresh in your mind.

8 As you plan your community celebrations and your endings, what will they look like for individuals, parents, groups, classes, year groups or as a whole school?

9 What do you want your children to experience, remember and feel as you end well together?

10 Make the most of your summer break! Make memories that you'll look back on fondly when it all starts again.

NOTES – My musings . . .

August

August – Part A

REST. . . .

Be rested

*****

 REFLECT:

How do you rest and become replenished?
How easy do you find it to rest?

August – Part B

And plan . . .
and liaise . . .

with other external professionals who don't have holidays when you
do and still require answers to questions and information being sent;

DOI: 10.4324/9781003333753-13

liaise with the local authority about funding for children that has still not been confirmed even though you kept to all the timeframes and tried your darndest to ensure it might be before the end of term, but you still haven't heard and you're still waiting, and if you're still waiting that means there are tentative plans you've put in place for September but none of them can be set in stone until we actually know ... and if we're waiting to know, that means staff are waiting to know, and parents are also waiting to know; and liaise with parents who are increasingly worried about their children's return to school, and although you've had so many conversations together and made so many preparations there's always another question that pops up ...

and discover ... that a new child who's just arrived in the area in August will now be coming to your school and no one knew until just now, and now you need to think about everything that they need and how you're going to make that happen ...

and do ... all the things you just didn't quite get round to doing before the end of term.

etc. etc. etc. ...

Even as we rest, we anticipate school's return, we anticipate reconnection. It's the getting ready for a kind of gathering up, a coming together. Colleagues catching up after the holidays, parents and children connecting together again in the playground, and people being met with welcome. Welcome back.

This is what we plan for. Whether people have had a whale of a time, exploring new experiences and places, or just some kind of mundanity to endure, and everything in between, our welcome is always warm. And what comes to mind are scenes from old tales where scattered peoples return, and the community is restored to a living, breathing, connected, thing where each actively takes part in a combined story. We make preparations to offer our welcome, we lay the table, set out the menu, we invite old guests as well as new, as our community starts to return.

Be our guest

*****

REFLECT:

How do you feel when you are genuinely welcomed by others?

What is it that particularly makes you feel welcome?

How do you create a welcoming community for all in your setting?

Monthly musings

August – holiday time

Finally the holidays are here. You've made it, even if you're crawling on your hands and knees, you've made it. Even though there may have been times where you didn't know if you would, you've made it.

1 Celebrate!
2 What have been some of your best holiday experiences in the past and why? Are there ways in which you can recreate elements of them this year?
3 What's on your bucket list to do this holiday? Plan small things to do as markers to look back on, so that you don't get to the end in a few weeks and wonder where it's all gone.
4 Don't take on board others' quips about how long the summer break is. You only fully know the craziness of the jobs we do if you work in a school! The truth is, we all need a good break to even begin to recharge.
5 As you begin to unwind from the stress of the previous weeks, think again about what you brought to the children and families you worked with.
6 Make sure you rest. No doubt the run-up to the end of term was manic and your body and mind need time and space to be replenished. What does that look like for you?
7 Don't let guilt about unfinished things rob you of rest and relaxation. Because we care about what we do, this can easily linger without us even realising. Identify the feeling and plan for how and when you'll tackle those things so that you don't become overwhelmed.
8 Find out what works best for you . . . finishing things you didn't get a chance to do at the start of the holidays while things are still fresh in your mind, or taking a break and tying up loose ends once you're more rested?

9 Limit what school preparation you do over the holidays. Get ahead of the game, be prepared for the start of the new term, but find a balance. We're in the kinds of jobs that can completely take over our lives if we let them. Learn to recognise the tension that our jobs and all we're expected to do are pretty much always bigger than our capacity.

10 Recall the good things about your summer before you head back into school.

NOTES – My musings . . .

Epilogue

Pippa McLean

So, one year draws to an end before another one begins. We rest, we take stock and get good to go again . . . and the cycle continues. One typical year after another, with an occasional atypical one in between. For any of us who have been in schools for a while, we'll recognise again and again the same kinds of frustrations and joys as we continue to hold our aspirations high and press into the work of inclusion.

If you're not careful you can get complacent or become cynical with what might seem to be the same old same old, or the echoes of what has gone before, and without even realising it fail to see the individual faces or hear the individual stories . . . and if this happens similar children and similar parents become somehow amalgamated in our memories, with the danger of losing sight of the person, the face, the name. The problem remains that in society, children with additional needs or SEND can still sometimes be bunched into categories that tend to inhibit, restrict and anonymise, which means people often don't see each other properly. They don't see the individual, the uniqueness of their strengths, their personalities and characters.

And oh, the characters! When you hear a good story, what you remember is how the author captured the very essence of the person, so that you lived and breathed the story with them, so that your story ran alongside theirs. We all have our own diaries; our own stories to tell. Stories of children and families we have known, children and families we have believed in, children and families we have cheered on, with all the frustrations and joys along the way. . . . We are to tell stories that capture the very essence of them; stories that inspire and spur others on to catch the passion of inclusion.

We still have a long way to go. The race is not run yet. We are to always champion inclusion. To champion each face, each name, each story, each journey, because although the challenges we face may feel familiar or typical as we see them come round again, the children we meet are not typical at all. Each are extraordinarily unique with their own stories to tell.

So, we keep the rhythm going, the beating of our hearts as well as the attention of our minds, and as each cycle begins again, we see new faces, new children, new parents; we hear new stories, take part in new journeys, entertain new ideas; we follow new guidance, new legislation . . . but it's always the age-old story of seeing the one. Each and every one.

If we really are the greatest resource in the room, with all the reality of good days and bad days thrown in, it matters who we are. It matters that we do the work of self-reflection, and consider what we bring to each story. Not that we somehow strive to be superhuman, but that we continue to have passion for the task at hand. It matters what we leave behind, and how people feel when we're in the room. It matters the things we remember and the stories we tell. It matters that we put our hearts and minds to the task. It matters because children and families matter.

The heart and mind rhythm of inclusion beats on . . .

It matters.

Index

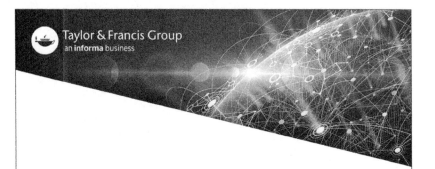